FOURTH ASSESSMENT PA

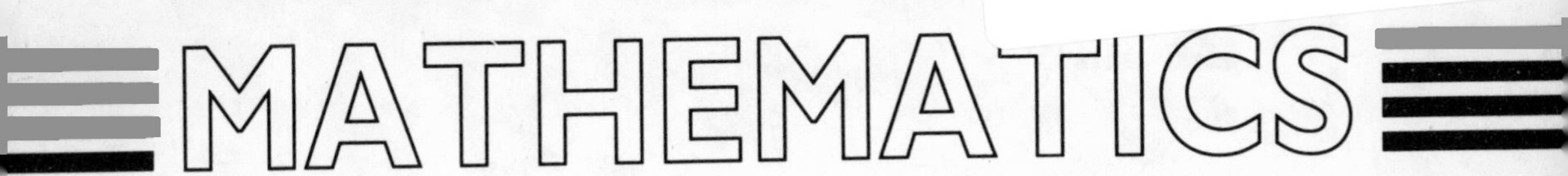

ANSWER BOOK

J M BOND

Nelson

Paper 1

Here is a pie chart which shows how Joanna spent yesterday evening between 6 p.m. and 8 p.m.

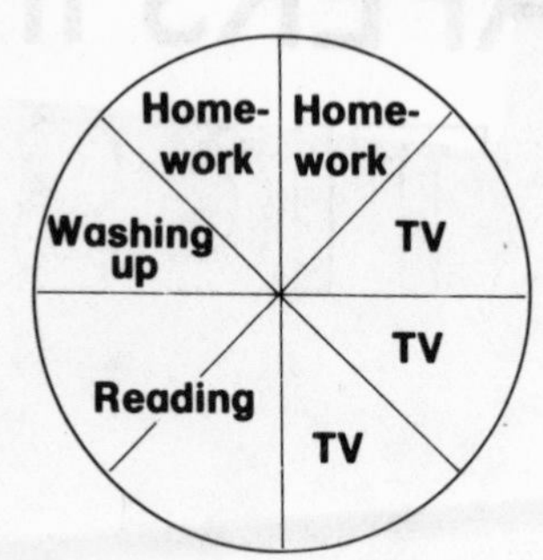

1–4 She was watching T.V. for $\frac{3}{4}$ hour, doing homework for $\frac{1}{2}$ hour, reading for $\frac{1}{2}$ hour and washing up for $\frac{1}{4}$ hour

5 What is the average (mean) of the following numbers? 7 4 6 8 5 ... 6

6 If the mean is 4, what is the missing number? 3 2 7 and ... 4

7 If the mean is 3, what is the missing number? 2 4 6 2 and ... 1

8 Make 999 twenty times as large. ... 19 980

9 $1\frac{1}{2} \times 2\frac{1}{2} = 3\frac{3}{4}$

10 $\frac{9}{10} \div \frac{27}{20} = \frac{2}{3}$

In each of the following lines underline the smallest number and put a ring round the largest number.

11	$\frac{5}{8}$	$\frac{3}{4}$	$\frac{7}{8}$	$\frac{1}{2}$	
12	3.07	3.7	37	3.007	0.307
13	$\frac{15}{3}$	$\frac{12}{6}$	$\frac{27}{9}$	$\frac{8}{2}$	$\frac{10}{10}$
14	0.125	$\frac{1}{2}$	0.25	$\frac{7}{8}$	0.75
15	$\frac{3}{4}$ of 12	$\frac{5}{7}$ of 14	$\frac{2}{3}$ of 9	$\frac{2}{5}$ of 10	$\frac{1}{2}$ of 16

16 Write in figures: one hundred and two thousand and twenty-one. ... 102 021

17–20

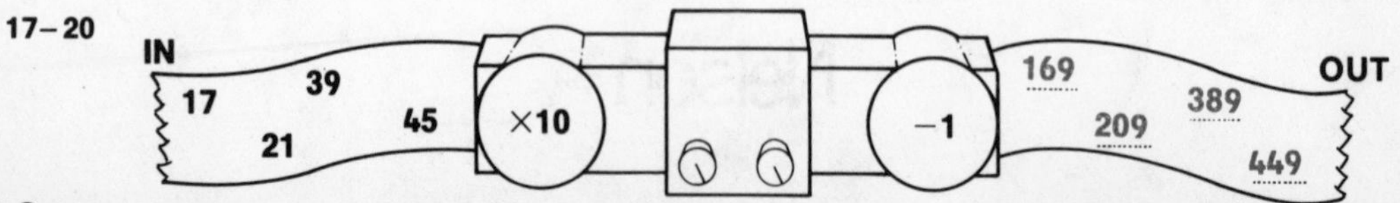

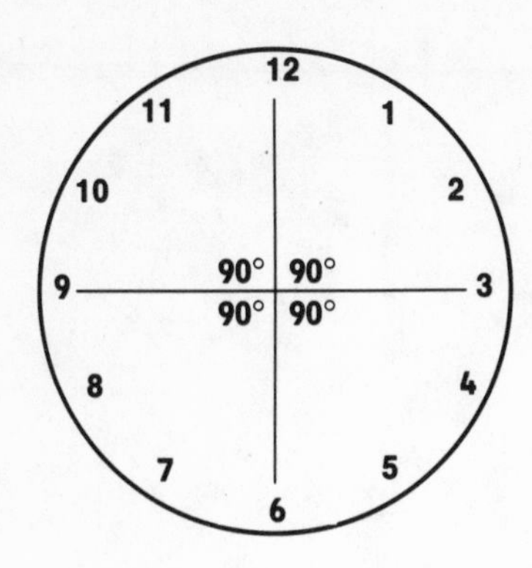

What is the size of the smaller angle:

21 between 1 and 3? 60°

22 between 2 and 7? 150°

23 between 7 and 11? 120°

24 between 8 and 9? 30°

25 between 4 and 10? 180°

26 $(7 \times 8) + 5 = 61$

27 $8 \times (7 - 3) = 32$

28 $(9 \times 12) - 2 = 106$

29 $6 \times (11 - 5) = 36$

Our ordinary numbers are called Arabic numbers. Turn these Roman numbers into Arabic numbers.

30 VIII = 8   31 XIV = 14   32 XVI = 16   33 IX = 9

34–36 Write the times which are a quarter of an hour before the following:

22.00 21.45   11.05 10.50   13.10 12.55

37–39 36 articles are shared among A, B and C in the ratio of 1:3:5. How many has A? 4 B has 12 C has 20

40–43 Write the set of fractions less than 1 which have a denominator of 5. $\frac{1}{5}, \frac{2}{5}, \frac{3}{5}, \frac{4}{5}$

44 It takes me 27 minutes to walk to school. What time must I leave home if I have to be at school by 5 minutes past nine? 08.38

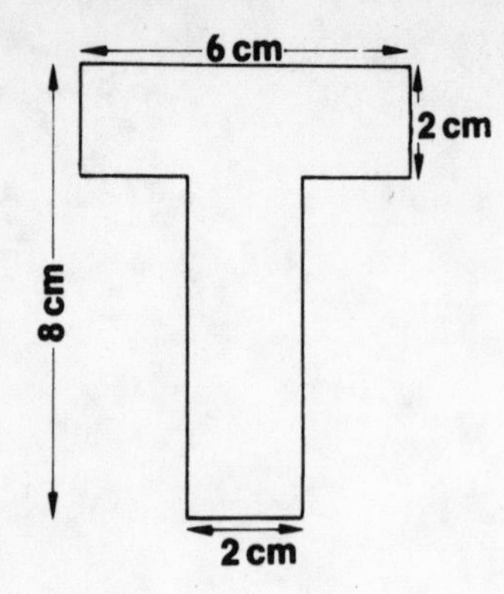

45 What is the area of this figure? 24 cm^2

46 What is its perimeter? 28 cm

Here is a ready reckoner. Use it for finding the cost of several bottles of Squish. Each bottle costs 13p.

1 bottle	13p	8 bottles	104p
2 bottles	26p	9 bottles	117p
3 bottles	39p	10 bottles	130p
4 bottles	52p	20 bottles	260p
5 bottles	65p	30 bottles	390p
6 bottles	78p	40 bottles	520p
7 bottles	91p	50 bottles	650p

47 14 bottles will cost £1.82 or 182p

48 22 bottles will cost £2.86 or 286p

49 31 bottles will cost £4.03 or 403p

50 44 bottles will cost £5.72 or 572p

Paper 2

Divide each of these numbers by 10.

1 78·65 7·865

2 6·54 0·654

3 467·5 46·75

4 0·123 0·0123

5–8 Work out these sums, and then put them in order - the one with the largest quotient first, the second largest next and so on.

A $7\overline{)315}$ = 45 B $8\overline{)392}$ = 49 C $7\overline{)329}$ = 47 D $9\overline{)387}$ = 43

B .... C .... A .... D ....

9–10 In a school 6 out of every 11 children are girls. If there are 407 children in the school there are:

185 .... boys and 222 .... girls.

Here are some of Charlotte's exam marks. Can you turn them into percentages?

	Subject	Charlotte's mark	Possible mark	Percentage
11	Maths	36	40	90
12	History	17	20	85
13	English	23	25	92
14	French	48	60	80

Here are some of Peter's percentages. Write down his actual marks.

	Subject	Peter's mark	Possible mark	Percentage
15	Maths	24	40	60
16	History	18	20	90
17	English	21	25	84
18	French	51	60	85

There are six balls, numbered 1 to 6, in a bag.

19 What chance is there I will draw out an even-numbered ball? 1 in 2

20 What chance is there that I will draw out the 5? 1 in 6

21 What chance is there that I will draw out an odd-numbered ball? 1 in 2

There are 240 children in a school. 105 children like football, 94 children like cricket and 63 children like neither game. Enter this information in the Venn diagram.

22–24 Ch = set of children
F = set of children who like football
C = set of children who like cricket

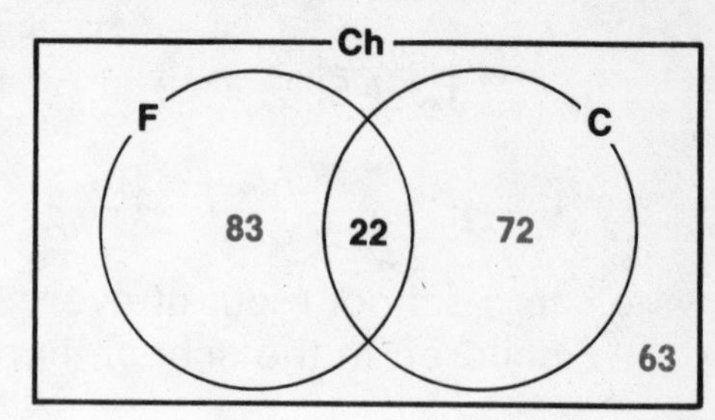

25 How many children in the school don't like football? 135

26 How many children in the school don't like cricket? 146

27 What number is midway between 18 and 42? 30

28 What number is midway between 19 and 53? 36

29 Find the area of a square whose perimeter is 12 cm. 9 cm²

Complete the following chart:

	Speed	Time taken	Distance
30	40 km/h	$1\frac{1}{2}$ hours	60 km
31	40 km/h	2 hours	80 km
32	60 km/h	$1\frac{1}{2}$ hrs or 1 hr 30 mins	90 km

Some places are ahead of our time and others are behind our time.

Austria is +1 hour

Cyprus is +2 hours

Hong Kong is +8 hours

Japan is +9 hours

When it is midday in London it is:

33 21.00 in Japan

34 13.00 in Austria

35 14.00 in Cyprus

36 20.00 in Hong Kong

When it is 15.00 in Japan it is:

37 06.00 in London

38 14.00 in Hong Kong

39 $\frac{5}{8} + \frac{7}{16} = 1\frac{1}{16}$

40 $7 - 4\frac{2}{9} = 2\frac{7}{9}$

Some marbles are shared between Tom and Matthew in the ratio of 5:4.

41 If Matthew receives 16 Tom will get ...20...

42 If they shared them equally Matthew would get ...18...

Write these fractions as decimals:

43 $4\frac{1}{2}$	44 $3\frac{1}{4}$	45 $7\frac{1}{10}$	46 $3\frac{9}{100}$
...4·5...	...3·25...	...7·1...	...3·09...

47
```
  887
  998
+ 776
 ----
 2661
```

48
```
  378
×   9
 ----
 3402
```

49
```
      234
12 ) 2808
```

50
```
   456
×   35
 -----
 15960
```

Paper 3

1–4

Which of the numbers in this shape is 2^3? ...8...

Which is 5^2? ...25...

Which is 3^2? ...9...

Which is 6^2? ...36...

5–15 Complete this timetable for Merrywell School. There are five lessons each 35 minutes in length, with a "break" of 15 minutes after the third lesson.

	Begins	Ends
1st lesson	09.10	09.45
2nd lesson	09.45	10.20
3rd lesson	10.20	10.55
Break	10.55	11.10
4th lesson	11.10	11.45
5th lesson	11.45	12.20

16 What is the number nearest to 5000, but smaller than it, into which 38 will divide without a remainder? ...4978...

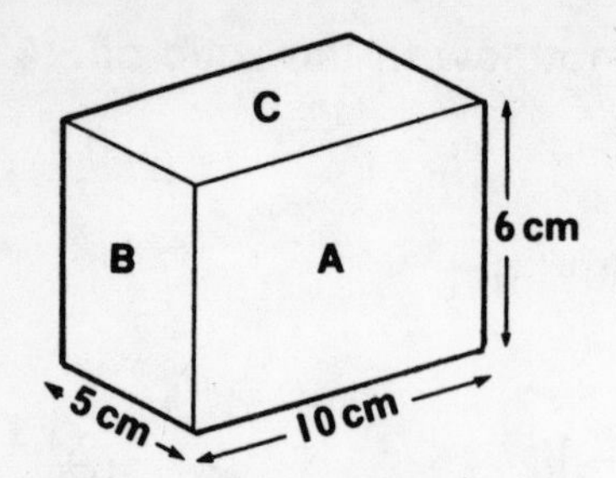

17–19 What is the area of:

side A? 60 cm² side B? 30 cm² side C? 50 cm²

20–22 What is the perimeter of:

side A? 32 cm side B? 22 cm side C? 30 cm

23 $2 \times \Delta = 4 \times 5$

$\Delta =$ 10

24 $\otimes \times 3 = 36 \div 3$

$\otimes =$ 4

25 $5 \times \square = 27 - 2$

$\square =$ 5

26 $\bigcirc \times 4 = 10 + 10$

$\bigcirc =$ 5

27–28 Alan is eleven years old and Emma is nine. They are given £4.80 to be shared between them in the ratio of their ages.

Alan will get £2.64 Emma will get £2.16

29 If 11 articles cost £7.37 what would be the cost of 8 similar articles? £5.36

Find the area of these triangles. The area of a triangle $= \frac{1}{2}$(base x height)
Scale: 1 square = 1 cm²

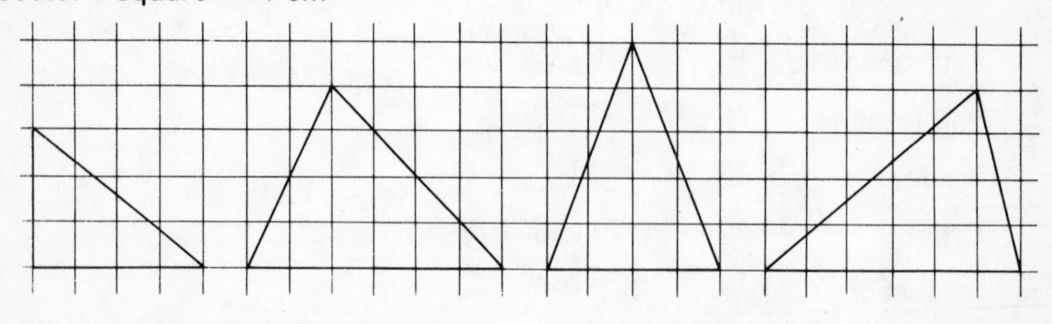

30 6 cm² **31** 12 cm² **32** 10 cm² **33** 12 cm²

At our car park the charges are as follows:

Up to 1 hour	50p
Over 1 hour and up to 2 hours	75p
Over 2 hours and up to 3 hours	£1.00
Over 3 hours and up to 4 hours	£1.50
Over 4 hours and up to 5 hours	£2.00
Over 5 hours and up to 6 hours	£2.50
Over 6 hours and up to 7 hours	£3.00
Over 7 hours and up to 8 hours	£3.50

34 Miss Short parks her car at 12.30 p.m. and collects it at 4 p.m. How much will she have to pay? £1.50

35 Mrs. Rowland's car is at the car park from 9.15 a.m. to 11.30 a.m. She will be charged £1.00

36 Mr. Read's car is at the car park from 2.40 p.m. to 6.30 p.m. He will have to pay £1.50

37 How much will Mr Davies have to pay if his car is left at the car park from 8.45 a.m. to 4.30 p.m.? £3.50

VAT (Value Added Tax) is charged at $17\frac{1}{2}\%$ on some goods. This means that a £100.00 article would have a tax of £17.50 added to its cost. Complete the table below.

	Price before VAT	VAT	Total cost
38–39	£200·00	£35·00	£235·00
40–41	£400·00	£70·00	£470·00
42–43	£100·00	£17·50	£117·50

44

	m	cm
	4	72
+	3	39
	8	11

45

	m	cm
	6	2
−	3	8
	2	94

46

	m	cm
	4	60
×		5
	23	0

Write correct to the nearest 100:

47 298 — 300

48 347 — 300

49 503 — 500

50 1074 — 1100

Paper 4

Fill in the gaps.

1–5

	Length	Width	Perimeter
Rectangle 1	18 cm	2 cm	40 cm
Rectangle 2	12 cm	3 cm	30 cm
Rectangle 3	9 cm	4 cm	26 cm
Square 1	6 cm	6 cm	24 cm

6 How many times can 28 be subtracted from 1316? 47 times

In each line put a ring round the correct answer.

7	0·1 × 0·1	= 0·2	0·02	(0·01)	0·1	1·1
8	10% of 40	= 8	5	80	20	(4)
9	10 − 9·99	= 0·9	(0·01)	1·00	1·1	1·9
10	0·207 ÷ 0·3	= 0·9	0·09	(0·69)	0·66	0·23
11	1·1 × 1·1	= (1·21)	1·11	11·1	2·2	1·01
12	567 ÷ 100	= 56 700	0·567	56·7	(5·67)	5670

13 The product of 2 numbers is 1260. One of the numbers is 35. What is the other number? 36

Fill in the missing figures in the sums below.

14–17

```
   4 3 6 5
   2 7 8 1
 + 3 4 5 7
 ---------
 1 0 6 0 3
```

18–20

```
   1 0 7 1
 −   2 8 5
 ---------
     7 8 6
```

21

```
   3 4 5
 ×     7
 -------
 2 4 1 5
```

Find the value of x in the following equations.

22 $3x = 10 - 1$

$x =$ 3

23 $4x - x = 12$

$x =$ 4

24 $2x + x = 6$

$x =$ 2

25 $3x + x = 11 + 1$

$x =$ 3

Some children were asked which kind of films they liked. 28 liked horror films, 27 liked westerns, and 20 liked comedies. Using this information complete the Venn diagram below.

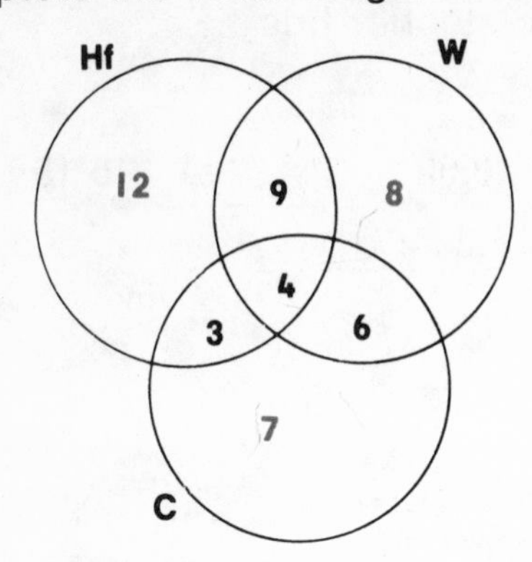

Hf = Horror films
W = Westerns
C = Comedies

26 How many like both Westerns and comedies? ....10....

27 How many like both horror films and comedies? ....7....

28 ....13.... children like both horror films and Westerns.

29 How many children like all three types of films? ....4....

30 How many like Westerns but not comedies and horror films? ....8....

31 How many like horror films but not comedies or Westerns? ....12....

32 How many don't like Westerns or horror films but like comedies? ....7....

33 How many don't like horror films? ....21....

34 How many don't like comedies? ....29....

35 How many don't like Westerns? ....22....

36 How many children were asked about these films? ....49....

Multiply each of these numbers by 10.

37 3·77 ....37·7....

38 46·5 ....465....

39 0·126 ....1·26....

40 0·027 ....0·27....

41 49 ....490....

42 567 ....5670....

43 0·0023 ....0·023....

Alan has half as many sweets as Brian, and Christopher has one third as many as Brian. Altogether they have 44 sweets.

44–46 Alan has 12 , Brian has 24 and Christopher has 8

Turn these times into a.m. or p.m. times.

47 05.05 5.05 a.m.

48 12.45 12.45 p.m.

49 20.02 8.02 p.m.

50 15.15 3.15 p.m.

Paper 5

Complete the following chart.

		Length	Width	Area
1	Rectangle 1	8 m	6 m	48 m^2
2	Rectangle 2	8 m	4 m	32 m^2
3	Rectangle 3	4 m	2·5 m	10 m^2
4	Rectangle 4	3 m	3·5 m	10·5 m^2
5	Rectangle 5	1·5 m	1·5 m	2·25 m^2
6	Rectangle 6	5 m	1·2 m	6 m^2
7	Rectangle 7	1·3 m	2·4 m	3·12 m^2

Find the area of these triangles. The area of a triangle = $\frac{1}{2}$(base × height)
Scale: 1 square = 1 cm^2

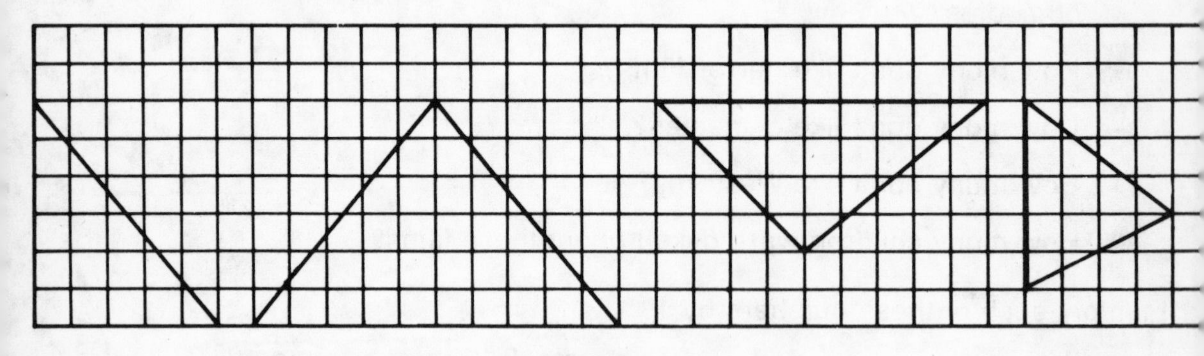

8 15 cm^2 **9** 30 cm^2 **10** 18 cm^2 **11** 10 cm^2

12 My watch loses a quarter of a minute every hour. If I put it right at midday, what time will my watch show at 8 p.m. that night? 7.58

13 I left home at 10.55 a.m. and arrived back at 5.24 p.m.
How long was I out? 6 hr 29 min

14–19 2 × ▼ = □

Complete this table.

□	2	4	6	8	10	12
▼	1	2	3	4	5	6

Reduce these prices by 10%

20 £50·00 £45·00 21 £110·00 £99·00 22 £250·00 £225·00

23 £40·00 £36·00 24 £30·00 £27·00 25 £280·00 £252·00

In an election 1140 people voted. Mr. Able and Mr. Brown together polled 675 votes, and Mr. Brown and Mrs. Khan together polled 862 votes.

26 How many votes did Mr. Brown poll? 397

27 278 people voted for Mr. Able.

28 465 voted for Mrs. Khan.

29–30 One day 10% of the children were away from school. If there were 360 children altogether, 324 children were present and 36 were absent.

31 A number multiplied by itself is 144. What is the number? 12

A Youth Club has 110 members. 27 of them can play the guitar, and 34 of them can play the piano. Fill in this information in two different ways in the Venn diagrams below.

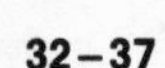

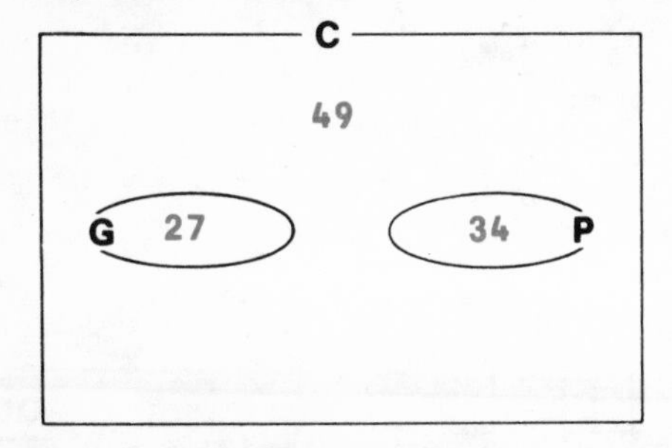

C = members of the Club G = those who play the guitar
P = those who play the piano

38 What number, when divided by 12, has an answer of 11 Rem 5? 137

39 A concert starts at 7.30 p.m. The first half of the programme lasts 1 hour 35 minutes, then there is an interval of 8 minutes. When does the second half of the concert begin? 9.13 p.m.

40 A rectangular field is three times as long as it is wide. If the perimeter is 0.8 km what is the length? 300 m

41 What is the width? 100 m **42** What is the area? 30 000 m^2

43 I have enough tinned food to last my two dogs for 18 days. If I got another dog how long would this food last? 12 days

44 Add the greatest to the smallest
565 656 556 655 566 665 1221

45 What number is halfway between 37 and 111? 74

46 By how much is the product of 19 and 13 greater than their difference? 241

Gary has half as many marbles as Daniel, and David has half as many as Gary. Together they have 84 marbles.

47 How many has Gary? 24

48 How many has Daniel? 48

49 How many has David? 12

50 What is the smallest number which, when divided by 3, 4 or 5, has a remainder of 1? 61

Paper 6

1–3

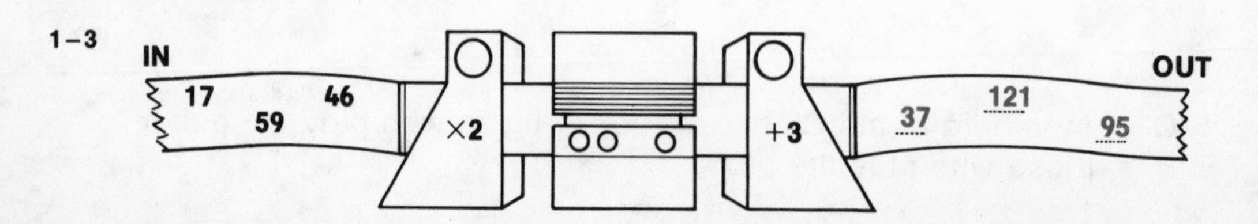

Here are five regular shapes – a triangle, a square, a pentagon, a hexagon and an octagon. (Regular shapes are those which have all their sides of equal length and whose angles are all equal.) Give the size of each angle formed at the centre of the shape.

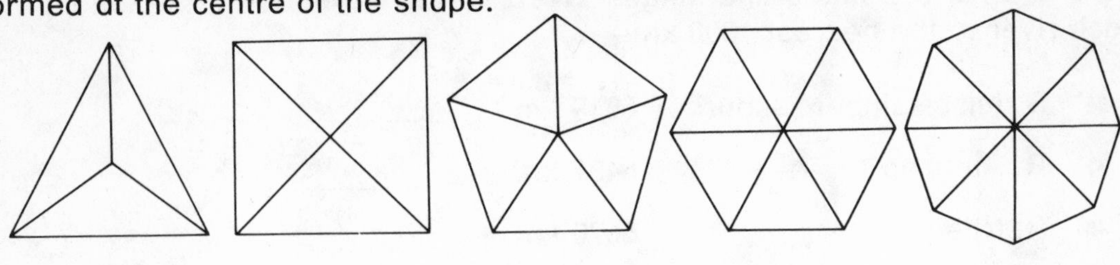

4 triangle 120°

5 square 90°

6 pentagon 72°

7 hexagon 60°

8 octagon 45°

Write the following lengths as metres and centimetres:

9 245 cm 2 m 45 cm

10 1342 cm 13 m 42 cm

11 12 345 cm 123 m 45 cm

Write the following distances as kilometres and metres:

12 1357 m 1 km 357 m

13 12 986 km 12 km 986 m

14 456 m 0 km 456 m

There are 30 children in Class 4. 60% of them are girls.

15–16 There are 18 girls and 12 boys.

17 Which number, when multiplied by 30, will give the same answer as 51 × 10? 17

18 Write the number which is 7 less than 2000. 1993

19–34 Insert signs in each space to make each line and column work out the given answer.

3	×	3	−	2	=	7
×		+		×		−
6	+	4	−	5	=	5
÷		−		−		×
2	×	5	−	4	=	6
=		=		=		=
9	×	2	−	6	=	12

35 If 9 articles cost £6.30, what will be the cost of 11 similar articles? £7.70

Here is a list of some of the longest rivers in the world. Write the length of each river to the nearest 1000 km.

36	R. Mississippi-Missouri	6019 km	6000 km
37	R. Amazon	6437 km	6000 km
38	R. Nile	6670 km	7000 km
39	R. Congo	4779 km	5000 km
40	R. Niger	4160 km	4000 km

41–46 Fill in the spaces with one of these signs $<$ $>$ $=$

$8 \times 9 = 6 \times 12$	$8 + 9 + 7 < 30 - 3$	0.5 m $>$ 45 cm
$2^3 < 3^2$	$12^2 = 144$	50 min $>$ $\frac{3}{4}$ hour

47–50 Write these times as you would see them on a digital watch.

1.05 pm	12.30 am	5.45 pm	11.01 am
13.05	00.30	17.45	11.01

Paper 7

Underline the correct answer in each line.

1	$0{\cdot}2 \times 0{\cdot}2$	= 0.4	4	40	0·04	0·004
2	$\frac{1}{2} + \frac{1}{4}$	= $\frac{2}{6}$	$\frac{3}{4}$	$\frac{2}{4}$	$\frac{2}{8}$	$\frac{1}{8}$
3	50% of 30	= 35	20	25	130	15
4	$10 \div \frac{1}{2}$	= 20	5	$10\frac{1}{2}$	$\frac{1}{20}$	$\frac{1}{5}$
5	$5 \div 0{\cdot}5$	= 0·1	0·01	100	10	0·001
6	$412 \div 4$	= 13	103	104	12	14
7	$\frac{1}{8} + \frac{1}{2}$	= $\frac{1}{16}$	$\frac{1}{10}$	$\frac{5}{8}$	$\frac{1}{2}$	$\frac{3}{8}$

8 Three buses leave the Bus Station at 7 a.m. Service A runs every 5 minutes, service B runs every 15 minutes, and service C runs every 12 minutes. At what time will all three services again start from the Bus Station at the same time? 8 a.m.

Here are two Venn diagrams. Fill in the information given below in both of the diagrams.

9–14

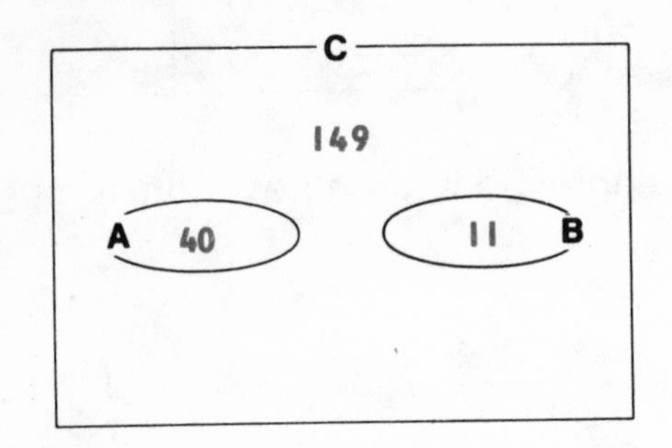

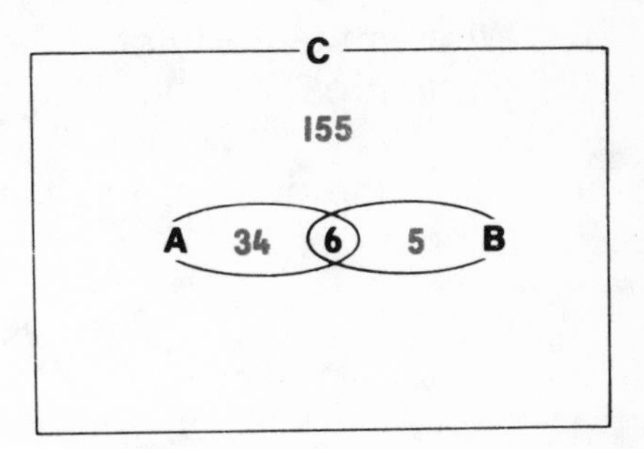

C = pupils in a school = 200 A = members of the choir = 40
B = members of the 1st Football XI = 11

15 What number, when multiplied by 10, has the same answer as 15 × 12? 18

Andrew has half as many marbles as Stuart, who has half as many as Meena. Together they have 140 marbles.

16–18 Meena has 80 marbles, Stuart has 40 and Andrew 20

Here is a record of attendances of 40 children for one week of the term.

	Mon.	Tues.	Wed.	Thurs.	Fri.
Morning attendances	36	33	37	34	35
Afternoon attendances	39	36	38	36	36

19–21 What was the (mean) average: morning attendance? 35

afternoon attendance? 37

daily attendance? 36

Multiply each of the numbers below by 10.

22 37·8 378

23 2·45 24·5

24 0·047 0·47

25 25·00 250

26 $7\frac{7}{8} + 5\frac{13}{16} =$ $13\frac{11}{16}$

27 $7\frac{1}{5} - 3\frac{11}{15} =$ $3\frac{7}{15}$

28–30 What is the area of:

the flag? 320 cm²

the cross? 128 cm²

the shaded part? 192 cm²

8 cm 4 cm 8 cm

6 cm

4 cm

6 cm

31 What is the perimeter of the flag? 72 cm

32 What is the perimeter of the cross? 72 cm

33–36 Name the angles. Are they right angles, acute angles, obtuse angles or reflex angles?

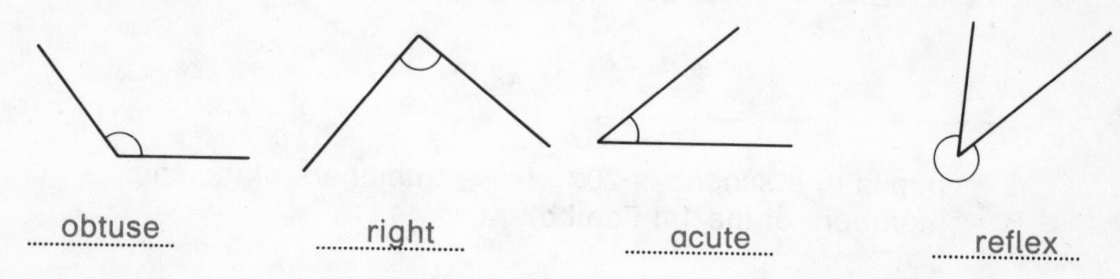

obtuse .... right .... acute .... reflex

37 If I travel at 60 km/h I do a journey in 10 minutes. How far do I go? 10 km

38 What is the difference between $\frac{1}{10}$ of 570 and $\frac{1}{3}$ of it? 133

Here is a large triangle made up of several small triangles. The top row consists of 1 triangle. In the top 2 rows there are 4 (or 2^2) triangles. In the top 3 rows there are 9 (or 3^2) triangles.

39 How many triangles are there in the 5 rows? 25

40 If there were 7 rows of triangles how many would there be? 49

41 In 11 rows there would be 121 triangles.

42 In 20 rows there would be 400 triangles.

43 Find the number nearest to 1000 which is divisible by 39. 1014

44 25 telegraph posts are spaced equally along the side of a road. If there is 85 metres between each pair of posts, how long is that stretch of road? 2040 m

45 A man's salary was £12 000. He is given a 5% increase. What is his new salary? £12,600

46 A cricketer's average score for 6 inning is 12 runs. What must he score in his next innings to make his average 13? 19

47 Add together 4·5 m, 16·7 m and 127·09 m 148·29 m

Complete the drawings below. The dotted line is the line of symmetry.

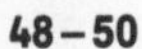
48–50

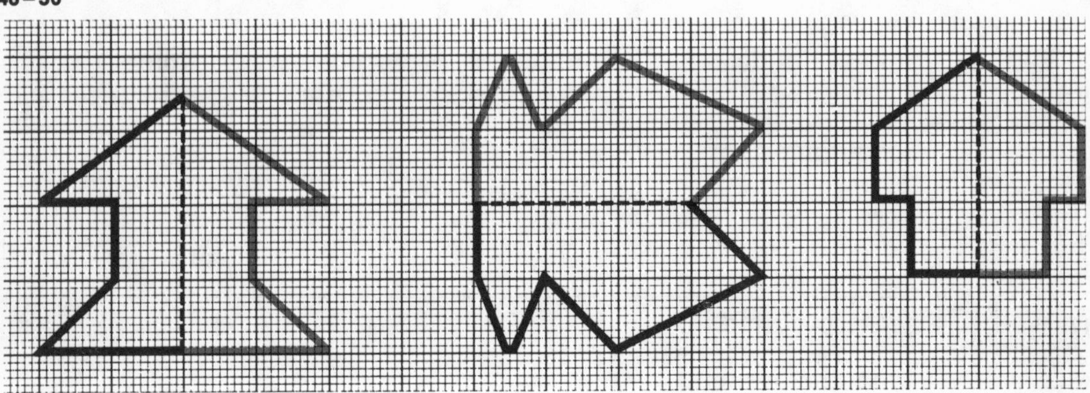

Paper 8

1 What is the difference between 0·255 tonnes and 128 kg? 0·127 tonnes or 127 kg

2 If a = 2 and b = 3 find the value of 4a − 2b 2

3 A book has 38 lines to each page. On which page will the 1000th line appear? 27

Turn these 12-hour times into 24-hour clock times.

4 10.10 a.m. 10.10

5 11.20 p.m. 23.20

6 1.01 a.m. 01.01

7 7.45 p.m. 19.45

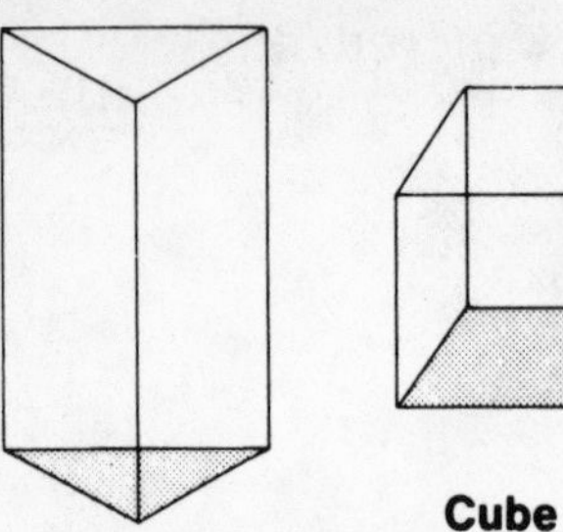

Triangular prism

Cube

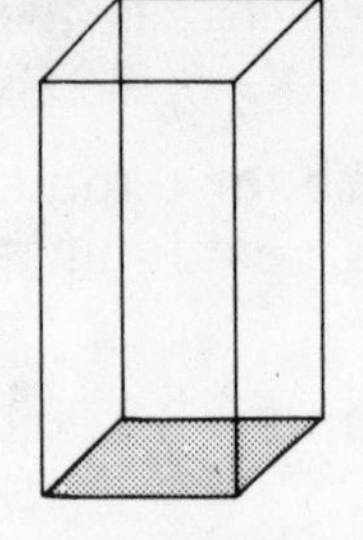

Square prism

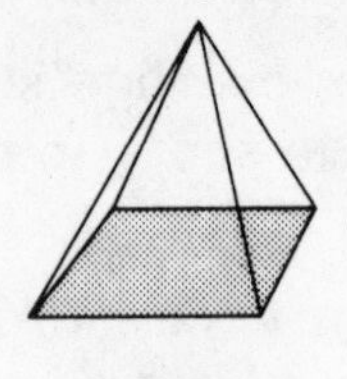

Square pyramid

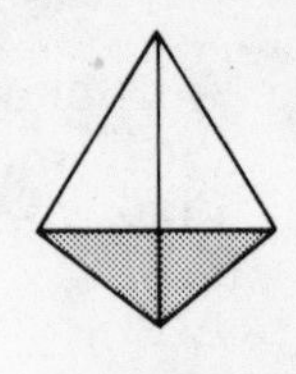

Triangular pyramid

	Name of solid	Number of faces	Number of vertices or corners	Number of edges
8–10	Triangular prism	5	6	9
11–13	Cube	6	8	12
14–16	Square prism	6	8	12
17–19	Square pyramid	5	5	8
20–22	Triangular pyramid	4	4	6

23 Mrs. Forgetmenot is 9 minutes late for the 9.42 a.m. train. How long will she have to wait for the next train which is due at 10.27 a.m.? 36 minutes

Local pubs took part in a "Clean the beach" campaign. Find out the percentage of members of each club which took part in this activity.

	Club	Numbers of members	Number who took part	Percentage
24	A	100	79	79
25	B	50	36	72
26	C	150	120	80
27	D	70	49	70
28	E	80	60	75

29 If $x = 5$ and $y = 2$ $\frac{4x}{5y} =$ 2

Complete this timetable for Workmore School. There are five lessons each 30 minutes long, with a "break" of 15 minutes after the third lesson.

		Begins	Ends
30–31	1st lesson	09.40	10.10
32–33	2nd lesson	10.10	10.40
34–35	3rd lesson	10.40	11.10
36–37	Break	11.10	11.25
38–39	4th lesson	11.25	11.55
40	5th lesson	11.55	12.25

Peter and Tim together have 36 marbles. Peter wins 2 from Tim, and then finds that he has 3 times as many as Tim.

41 How many did Peter have at first? 25

42 How many did Tim have at first? 11

Can you fill in the gaps, if £1·00 = 2400 Italian lire?

	Article	English money	Italian money
43	A toy	£1·50	3600 lire
44	A beach bag	£2·00	4800 lire
45	An ornament	50p	1200 lire
46	A clock	£5·50	13 200 lire

47 3 whole numbers multiplied together total 2475. Two of the numbers are 25 and 11. What is the third number? 9

There are 351 children in a school. There are 7 boys to every 6 girls.

48 How many boys are there? 189

49 How many girls are there? 162

50 A number multiplied by itself and then doubled is 242. What is the number? 11

Paper 9

Use these words to help you name the following shapes:
hexagon, square, parallelogram, rectangle, rhombus

1–5

rhombus .... hexagon .... parallelogram .... rectangle .... square ....

Temperatures, one day in February, were:

Chicago −3°	Montreal −10°	Singapore 31°
Cape Town 27°	Miami 26°	Toronto −5°

6 Which was the hottest of these places? Singapore

7-8 The coldest was Montreal. How much colder was it in Chicago than in Cape Town? 30°

9 The difference between Toronto and Miami was 31°

10 The difference between Singapore and Montreal was 41°

11 From the largest number which can be formed from the figures 3, 9, 7 and 2 take the smallest number. What is your answer? 7353

12 How many comics, each costing 35p, can be bought for £15.00? 42

13 How much money would be left over? 30p

14 In a certain sum Amanda multiplied by 7 instead of dividing by 7. Her answer was 6027. What should it have been? 123

Write the next two numbers in each line.

15–16	$3\frac{1}{2}$	$4\frac{1}{4}$	$4\frac{3}{4}$	$5\frac{1}{2}$	6	$6\frac{3}{4}$
17–18	100	90	81	73	66	60
19–20	47	52	58	65	73	82
21–22	2	5	11	20	32	47
23–24	2	4	14	16	26	28

25–26 The perimeter of a rectangular piece of paper is 48 cm. The length is 3 times the width. The length is 18 cm and the width 6 cm

27–31

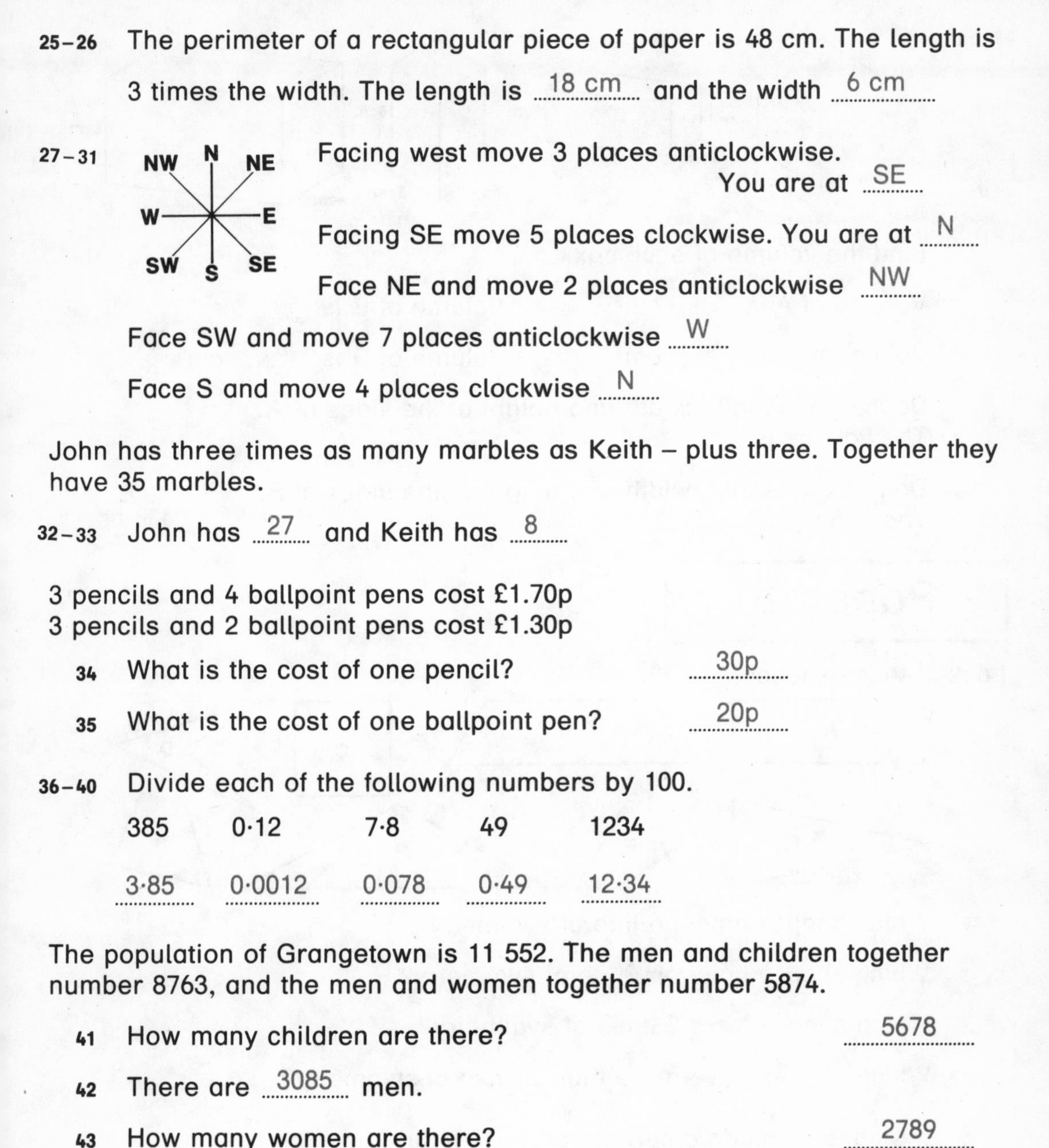

Facing west move 3 places anticlockwise. You are at SE

Facing SE move 5 places clockwise. You are at N

Face NE and move 2 places anticlockwise NW

Face SW and move 7 places anticlockwise W

Face S and move 4 places clockwise N

John has three times as many marbles as Keith – plus three. Together they have 35 marbles.

32–33 John has 27 and Keith has 8

3 pencils and 4 ballpoint pens cost £1.70p
3 pencils and 2 ballpoint pens cost £1.30p

34 What is the cost of one pencil? 30p

35 What is the cost of one ballpoint pen? 20p

36–40 Divide each of the following numbers by 100.

385	0·12	7·8	49	1234
3·85	0·0012	0·078	0·49	12·34

The population of Grangetown is 11 552. The men and children together number 8763, and the men and women together number 5874.

41 How many children are there? 5678

42 There are 3085 men.

43 How many women are there? 2789

44 How many minutes are there between 6.50 a.m. and 2 p.m.? 430

45–50

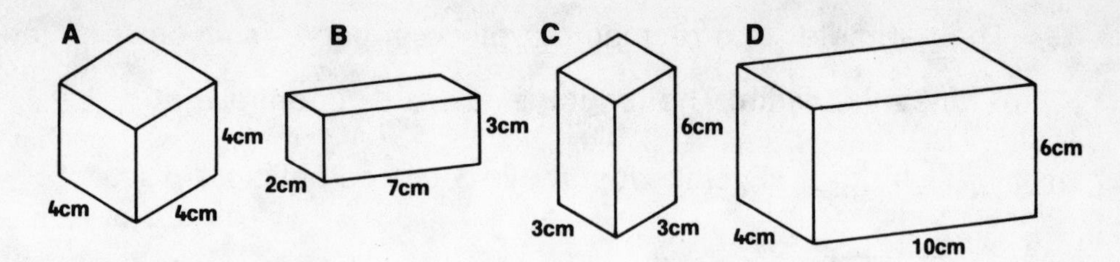

Find the volume of each box.

Volume of A is 64 cm^3 Volume of B is 42 cm^3

Volume of C is 54 cm^3 Volume of D is 240 cm^3

Double the length, width and height of the sides of A.
The volume is 512 cm^3

Double the length, width and height of the sides of B.
The volume is 336 cm^3

Paper 10

Look at these shapes.

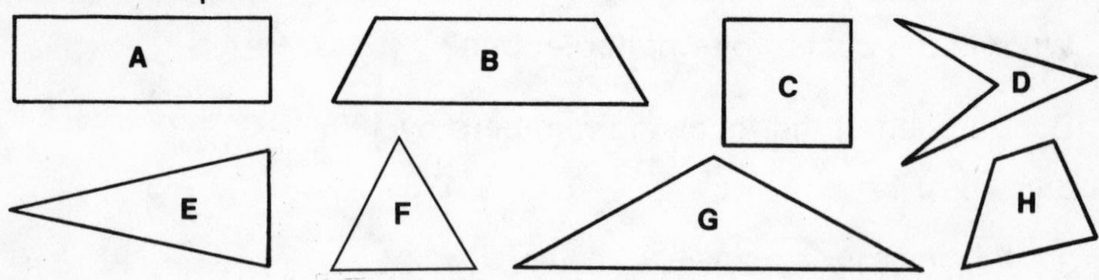

1–8 Which shapes have no line of symmetry? H

Which shapes have one line of symmetry? B, D, E, G

Which shapes have 2 lines of symmetry? A

Which shapes have more than 2 lines of symmetry? C, F

9 If 8 people can do a certain job in 10 hours, how long would it take 20 people to do the same job, working at the same speed? 4 hours

10 Find the average (the mean) of 7 11 4 6 2 6

11 36 posts were spaced evenly along a road 1·575 km long. What was the distance in metres between each pair of posts? 45 metres

Complete the following chart.

	Wholesale price (Price at factory)	Retail price (Price in shop)	Profit (Money made by shopkeeper)
12	£7.85	£9.22	£1.37
13	£14.76	£17.10	£2.34
14	£38.75	£44.42	£5.67
15	£17.37	£21.14	£3.77
16	£41.85	£50.04	£8.19
17	£54.89	£67.76	£12.87
18	£0.87	£1.05	£0.18

19–23 Plot the following co-ordinates on the chart and join them in the order you plot them.
(1,1) (1,4) (2,3) (3,4) (3,1)

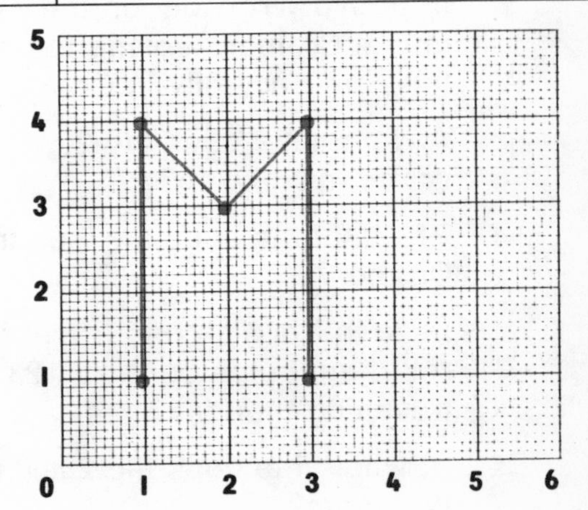

24 Which letter have you made? M

Emma, who is 8 years old, Richard who is 7, and Katie who is 5, share £10.00 in the ratio of their ages.

25–27 Emma gets £4·00, Richard gets £3·50 and Katie £2·50

28 What must be added to 375 g to make 1 kg? 625 g

29 How many packets, each holding 125 g, can be filled from a case holding 3 kg? 24

Write as fractions in their lowest terms.

30 3·8 $3\frac{4}{5}$

31 11.4 $11\frac{2}{5}$

32 11·002 $11\frac{1}{500}$

33 3·25 $3\frac{1}{4}$

34 6·5 $6\frac{1}{2}$

35 1·12 $1\frac{3}{25}$

Mr. and Mrs. Black took their three children from Longford to Burbridge by train. The tickets for the five people totalled £5.39. All the children travelled at half price.

36 How much was an adult ticket? £1.54

	Train A	Train B	Train C	Train D
Norwich	06.15	07.33	20.48 ↑	22.10 ↑
Wroxham	06.28	07.48	20.32	21.54
Worstead	06.35	07.55	20.24	21.47
North Walsham	06.45	08.02	20.19	21.41
Gunton	06.51	08.08	20.09	21.35
Cromer	↓ 07.04	↓ 08.21	19.57	21.23

37-38 Train D is the fastest and Train C the slowest.

39 If I leave Wroxham on the 7.48 train, and spend the day in Cromer, leaving there on the 19.57 train, how long am I actually in Cromer? 11 hr 36 min

40 At what time does the 20.19 train from North Walsham arrive in Norwich? 20.48

41 At what time does the 7.55 train from Worstead arrive in Cromer? 08.21

42 I live in Norwich and travel to Cromer on the 06.15 train, returning home on the 21.23 train. How long will I spend travelling that day? 1 hr 36 min

43 At what time does the 20.09 from Gunton reach Wroxham? 20.32

In a sale all goods were reduced by 20%. Complete the chart below.

	Ordinary price	Sale price
44	£20·00	£16·00
45	£35·00	£28·00
46	£60·00	£48·00
47	£180·00	£144·00
48	£55·00	£44·00
49	£40·00	£32·00
50	£275·00	£220·00

Paper 11

This graph represents the journeys of a cyclist and a motorist.

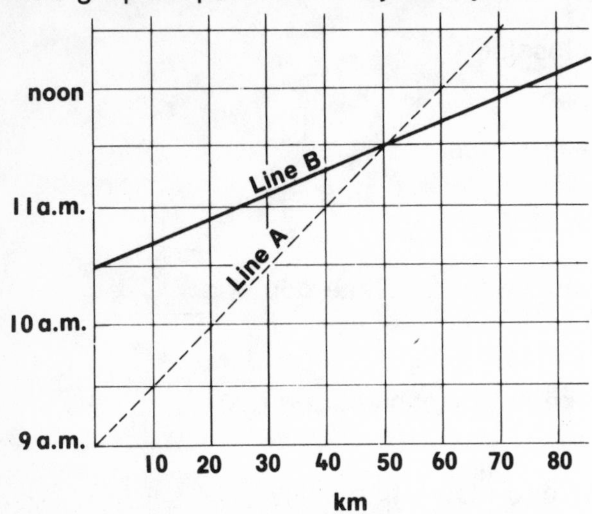

1 Which line represents the journey of the cyclist? Line A

2 At what speed was the cyclist travelling? 20 km/h

3 At what speed was the motorist travelling? 50 km/h

4 At what time did the motorist start his journey? 10.30 a.m.

5 At what time did the cyclist start? 9 a.m.

6 At what time did the motorist overtake the cyclist? 11.30 a.m.

7 How many km had the cyclist done when he was overtaken? 50 km

8 How many km had the cyclist done before the motorist started his journey? 30 km

9 What would be the approximate cost of 13 CDs at £4.98 each? £65

10 The average of 4 numbers is $10\frac{1}{2}$. If the average of 3 of them is 9 what is the 4th number? 15

Arrange in order of size, putting the largest first:

11–15 $\frac{1}{2}$ $\frac{2}{3}$ $\frac{5}{6}$ $\frac{3}{8}$ $\frac{3}{4}$

$\frac{5}{6}$ $\frac{3}{4}$ $\frac{2}{3}$ $\frac{1}{2}$ $\frac{3}{8}$

Some children in a Youth Club made this Venn diagram to show which type of music they prefer.

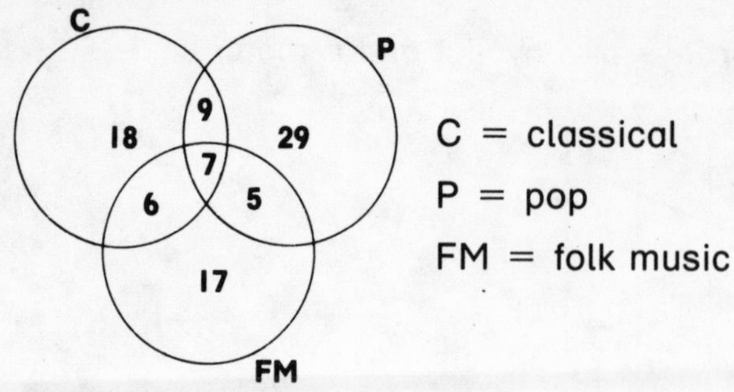

16–18 ...40... children like classical music, ...50... like pop and ...35... like folk music.

19 The number of children who like both classical and pop is ...16...

20 How many like classical music and also folk music? ...13...

21 How many like both folk music and pop? ...12...

22 How many children like all three types of music? ...7...

23 How many children don't like classical music? ...51...

24 How many don't like pop? ...41...

25 How many children don't like folk music? ...56...

26 How many children were there altogether? ...91...

27 $8\frac{5}{9} + 4\frac{2}{3} =$ ...$13\frac{2}{9}$...

28 $8\frac{2}{5} - 4\frac{11}{15} =$ ...$3\frac{2}{3}$...

29 $1\frac{3}{4} \times 1\frac{1}{5} =$ ...$2\frac{1}{10}$...

30 $29 \overline{)16472}$ = 568

31
```
   708
 × 407
288156
```

32
```
   day  hr
     1  11
5 )  7   7
```

Underline the correct answer.

33	$\frac{1}{8} + \frac{1}{4}$	=	$\frac{1}{12}$	$\frac{2}{12}$	$\frac{3}{8}$	$\frac{1}{4}$
34	2·00 − 1·77	=	0·33	0·23	3·77	1·23
35	0·3 × 0·3	=	0·09	0·6	0·06	0·33
36	3 ÷ 0·6	=	0·2	0·5	0·18	5

Fill in this chart:

		Circle 1	Circle 2	Circle 3	Circle 4
37–40	Diameter	$3\frac{1}{2}$	$4\frac{3}{4}$	5·5	$3\frac{7}{8}$
	Radius	$1\frac{3}{4}$	$2\frac{3}{8}$	2·75	$1\frac{15}{16}$

A cash box contains some coins to the value of £5.25. There are twice as many 5p s as 2p s, and twice as many 2p s as 1p s. So there are:

41 ...84... 5p coins 42 ...42... 2p coins 43 ...21... 1p coins

The ages of Grandad, Uncle John and Tom add up to 104 years. Grandad is twice as old as Uncle John and Uncle John is 4 times as old as Tom.

44–46 Grandad is ...64... years old, Uncle John is ...32... and Tom is ...8...

Divide each of the following numbers by 100.

47 34.2	48 8.6	49 274.6	50 3
0.342	0.086	2.746	0.03

Paper 12

1–5

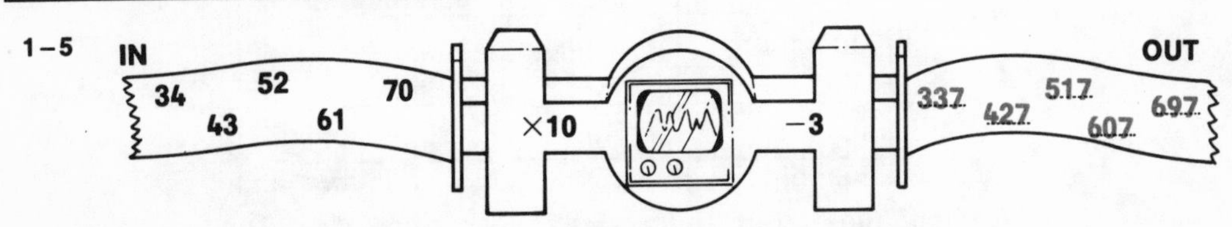

$5 \times 5 = 5^2$ and $2 \times 2 \times 2 = 2^3$. Now write these in shorthand.

6 $10 \times 10 \times 10 \times 10 =$ ...10^4...

7 $7 \times 7 \times 7 =$ ...7^3...

8 $5 \times 5 \times 5 \times 5 \times 5 =$ ...5^5...

9 $1 \times 1 \times 1 \times 1 \times 1 \times 1 =$ ...1^6...

10 $4 \times 4 \times 4 \times 4 =$ ...4^4...

11 $11 \times 11 \times 11 \times 11 \times 11 =$ ...11^5...

12 What number is $1 \times 1 \times 1 \times 1 \times 1 \times 1$? ...1...

13 Find the area of a hall which is 9 metres long and 7 metres wide. ...63 m^2...

14 What is the perimeter of the hall? ...32 m...

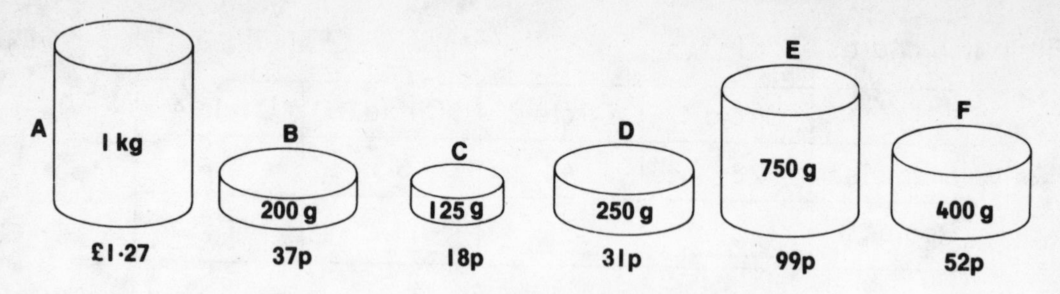

At the supermarket there were various sizes of Marvello.

15 Tin D was the best bargain.

16 Tin A was the second best.

17 Tin F was the third best.

18 Tin E was the fourth best.

19 Tin C was the fifth best.

20 Tin B was the most expensive way to buy Marvello.

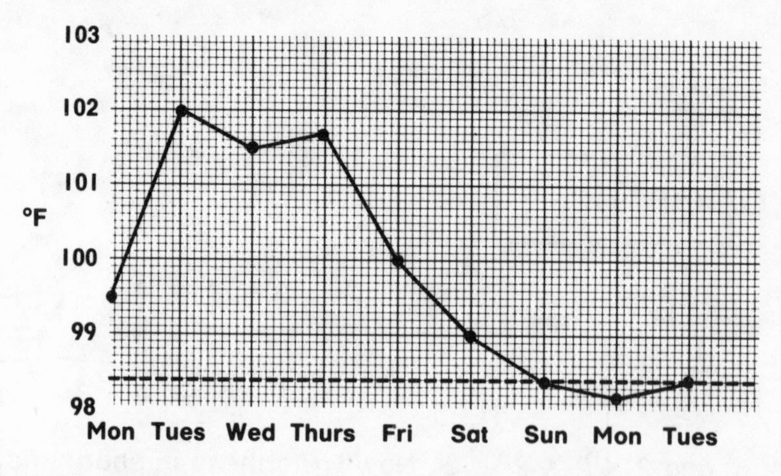

Here is Robin's temperature chart when he was ill. The dotted line shows the normal temperature of a person.

21 On how many days was his temperature above normal? 6

22 On how many days was his temperature below normal? 1

23 On which day do you think he was most ill? Tuesday

24 On which day do you think he started getting better? Thursday or Friday

25 What is a person's normal temperature? 98·4°F

26–31 In the end-of-term tests Felicity got the following marks.

Mathematics $\frac{54}{75}$ English $\frac{48}{60}$ History $\frac{13\frac{1}{2}}{20}$

French $\frac{25}{40}$ Geography $\frac{19\frac{1}{2}}{25}$ Art $\frac{7\frac{1}{2}}{10}$

Her best subject was English 2nd was Geography

3rd was Art 4th was Mathematics

5th was History 6th was French

Write the next two amounts in each line.

32–33	2	3	5	9	17	33	
34–35	5000	500	50	5	0·5	0·05	
36–37	1	$1\frac{1}{2}$	$2\frac{1}{2}$	3	4	$4\frac{1}{2}$	$5\frac{1}{2}$
38–39	0·6	0·7	0·8	0·9	1·0	1·1	
40–41	0·125	0·25	0·375	0·5	0·625	0·75	

There are 30 children in our class. We drew this Venn diagram to show how many of us belong to the Birdwatchers' Club, and how many belong to the Stamp Collectors' Club.

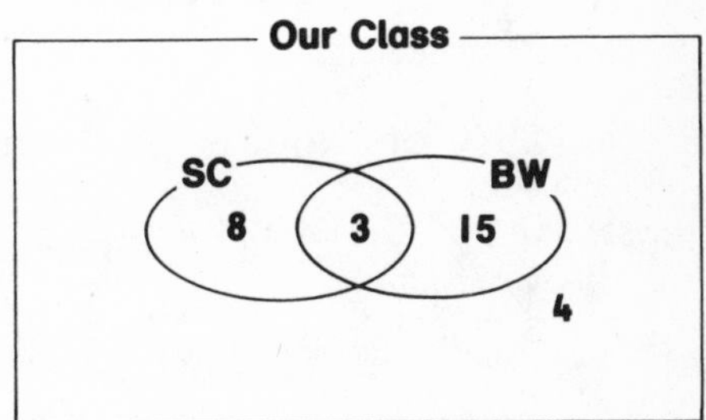

42 How many children belong to the Stamp Collectors' Club? 11

43 How many children belong to the Birdwatchers' Club? 18

44 How many belong to both Clubs? 3

45 How many children don't belong to the Stamp Collectors' Club? 19

46 How many don't belong to the Birdwatchers' Club? 12

47 How many children belong to one Club only? 23

48 How many don't belong to either of the Clubs? 4

Mum is 20 years older than Andrew, and 24 years older than Anne. The three ages total 73 years.

49 Mum is 39 years **50** Andrew is 19 years

Paper 13

Complete the figures below. The dotted line is the line of symmetry.

1–3

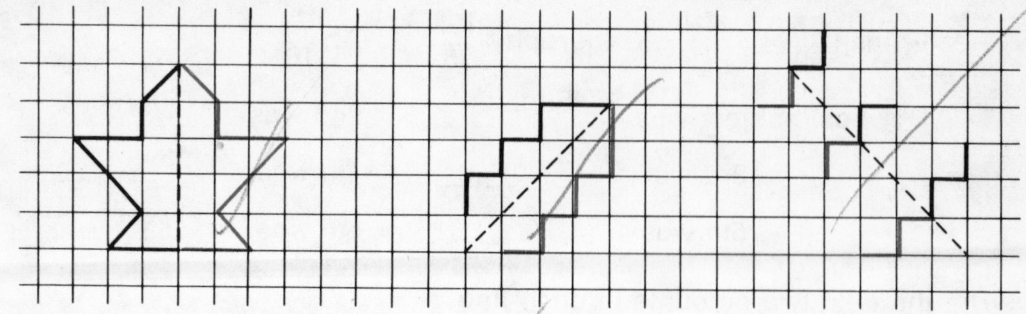

Underline the correct answer.

4	$\frac{1}{5} + \frac{2}{10}$	$= \frac{3}{15}$	$\frac{2}{5}$	$\frac{3}{10}$	$\frac{5}{10}$	$\frac{1}{5}$
5	$0{\cdot}49 \div 7$	= 7	0·7	0·07	70	700
6	20% of 35	= 7	8	20	15	25
7	$4^2 - 3^2$	= 1	2	3	7	9
8	$2^3 - 2^2$	= 1	2	3	4	5
9	25% of 1 metre	= 1 dm	1 cm	2 cm	25 cm	
10	$0{\cdot}1 \times 0{\cdot}1 \times 0{\cdot}1$	= 0·3	0·2	0·001	0·003	
11	$\frac{1}{3} + \frac{1}{6}$	$= \frac{2}{3}$	$\frac{1}{2}$	$\frac{1}{9}$	$\frac{2}{9}$	

Share £3·40 among Angela, Ben and Claire. For every 10p Angela gets, Ben gets 5p, and Claire gets 2p.

12–14 Angela gets £2·00, Ben gets £1·00 and Claire 40p

15 $\frac{3}{4}$ of a sum of money is £1·80. What is $\frac{1}{3}$ of it? 80p

16 Multiply 3·7 by itself, and then take 3.7 from the answer. 9·99

17 Add together 3·7, 2·95 and 0·187 6·837

18 Take 1·689 from 3·2 1·511

19 Divide 799 by 17 47

Multiply each of the numbers below by 10. Give your answers as whole numbers, or mixed numbers, the fractions to be in their lowest terms.

20 2.75 $27\frac{1}{2}$

21 38.2 382

22 0.125 $1\frac{1}{4}$

23 0.0875 $\frac{7}{8}$

This column graph shows the marks gained by some children in a test. The maximum mark was 100. One boy gained over 90 marks. $\frac{2}{5}$ of those who received between 80 and 90 marks were girls. $\frac{3}{4}$ of those who gained between 70 and 80 marks were boys. $\frac{1}{2}$ of those who got between 60 and 70 marks were girls. $\frac{1}{3}$ of those who gained between 50 and 60 marks were girls. $\frac{1}{2}$ of those who gained between 40 and 50 marks were boys.

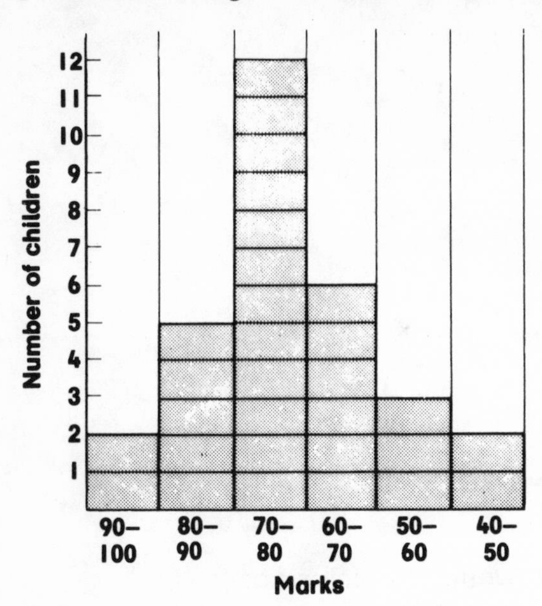

24 How many children took the test? 30

25 How many girls got over 90 marks? 1

26 How many boys received between 60 and 70 marks? 3

27 How many girls gained between 40 and 50 marks? 1

28 In the 80 to 90 mark range how many were boys? 3

29 In the 70 to 80 mark range how many girls were there? 3

30 How many boys gained between 50 and 60 marks? 2

Two friends, Alan and Barry, travel to a town which is 21 km away. Alan leaves home at 9.30 a.m. and walks there at an average speed of 6 km/h. Barry leaves home at 10.45 a.m. and cycles at an average speed of 14 km/h.

31 Who arrives at the town first? Barry

32 How long does it take him to travel there? 1 hr 30 min

33-34 Barry arrives at 12.15 p.m. and Alan at 1.00 p.m.

What is the order of rotational symmetry?

35

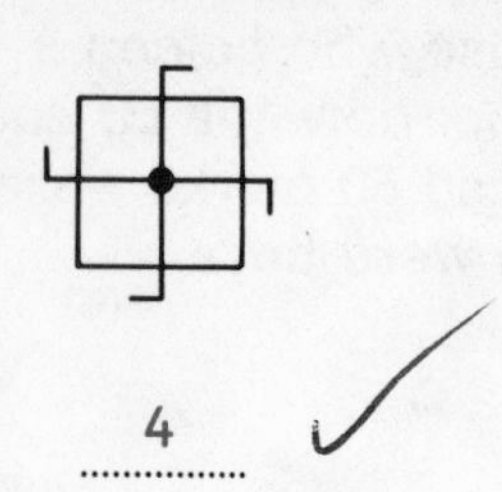

4 ✓

36

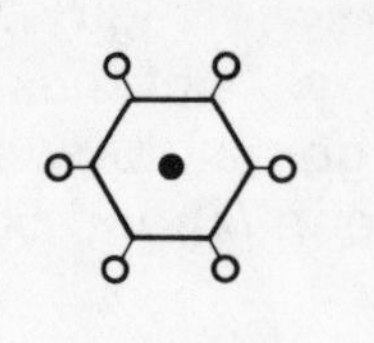

6 ✓

37

6 ✓

38

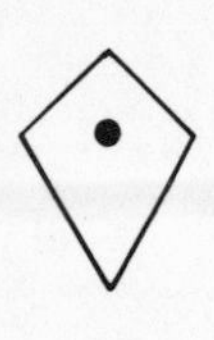

1 ✗

39

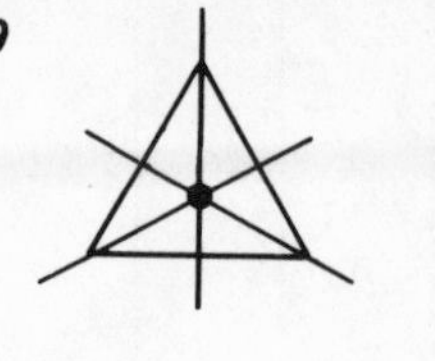

3 ✗

40

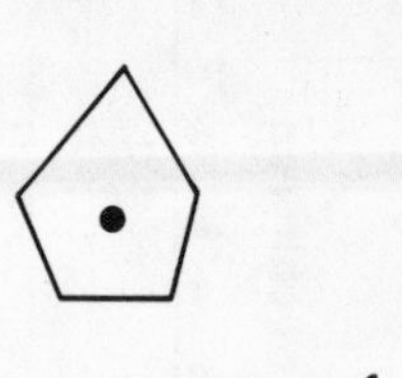

1 ✓

bad work

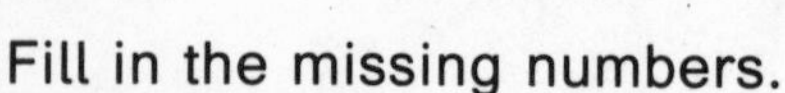

Fill in the missing numbers.

41 $\frac{4}{5} = \frac{20}{25}$ ✗ **42** $\frac{7}{11} = \frac{77}{121}$ ✗ **43** $\frac{4}{5} = \frac{32}{40}$ ✗ **44** $\frac{7}{8} = \frac{56}{64}$ ✗

45 $\frac{2}{7} = \frac{12}{42}$ ✗ **46** $\frac{3}{4} = \frac{36}{48}$ ✓

47 If 13 articles cost £1.56 what would 7 articles cost? £0.84

Share 39 sweets among Penny, Polly and Prue giving Penny 3 times as many as Polly, and Polly 3 times as many as Prue.

48–50 Penny has 27, Polly has 9 and Prue has 3

Paper 14

Complete this table.

1–3

60	144	72	132	120
5	12	6	11	10

4

```
   £
  0·38
×   11
  4·18
```

5

```
     £
   0.57
9)5.13
```

6

```
  1030
−  752
   278
```

Look at this graph and then answer these questions.

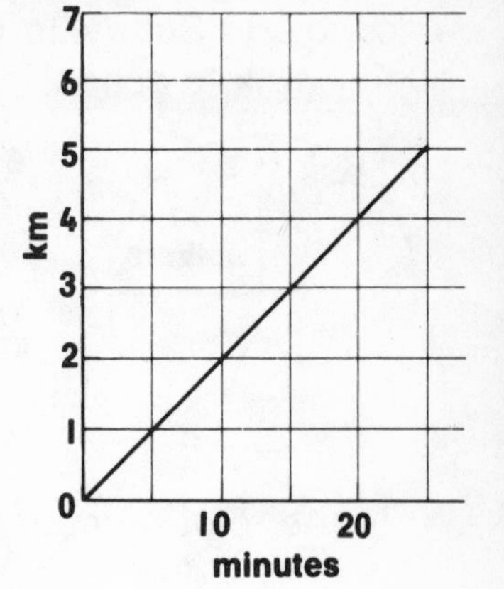

7 What is my speed in km/h? 12 km/h

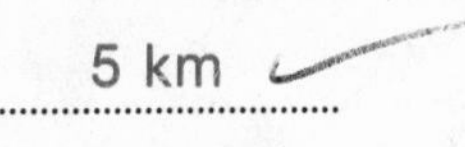

8 In 25 minutes how far would I go? 5 km

9 I'll do 2 km in 10 minutes

10 I'll do 1 km in 5 minutes

11 What number when multiplied by 25 gives the same answer as 45 × 40? 72

Solve these equations.

12–17 $3 + a = 15$ $\quad a = 12$

$x + 4 = 7$ $\quad x = 3$

$5 + a = 7$ $\quad a = 2$

$y - 7 = 9$ $\quad y = 16$

$b - 4 = 8$ $\quad b = 12$

$c - 1 = 5$ $\quad c = 6$

Which of these has the largest quotient?

18 A: $7 \overline{)896}$ = 128

19 B: $6 \overline{)786}$ = 131

20 C: $9 \overline{)1188}$ = 132

21 D: $4 \overline{)516}$ = 129

22 C has the largest quotient.

23 It takes me 19 minutes to walk home from school. If I leave school at 3.45 p.m. what time will I get home? 4.04 p.m.

24 How many minutes are there from 10.29 p.m. Monday to 2.05 a.m. Tuesday? 216

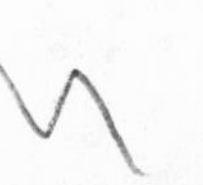

4 schools in Sandville made these pie charts which show how many of their pupils walk to school.

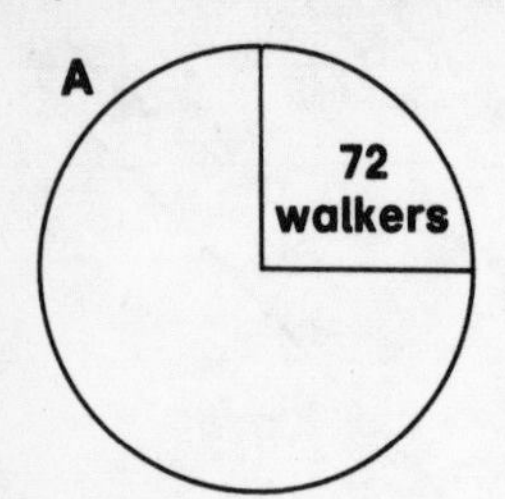

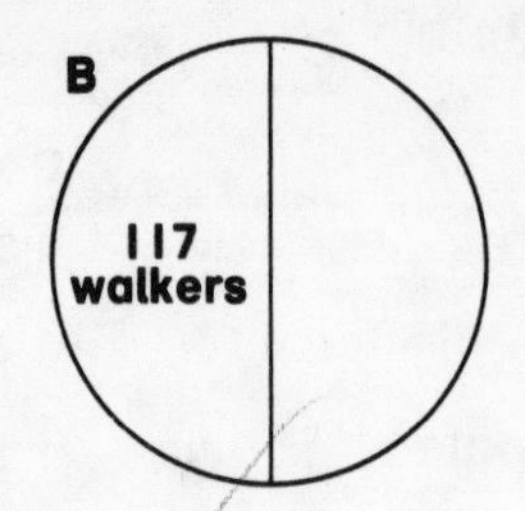

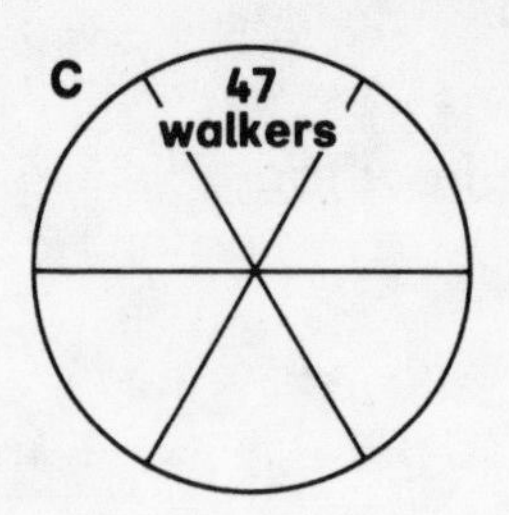

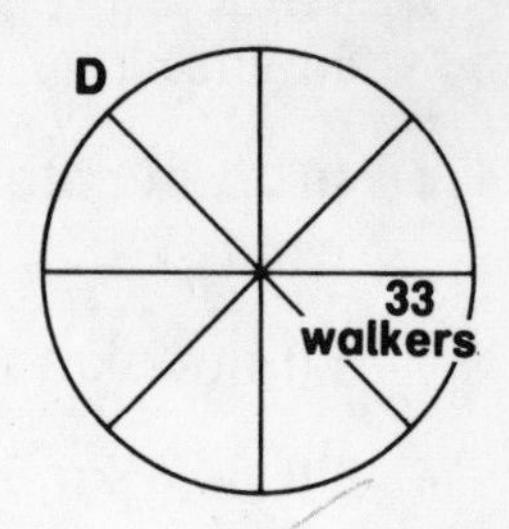

Write the total number of pupils in each school.

25 In School A 288

26 In School B 234

27 In School C 282

28 In School D 264

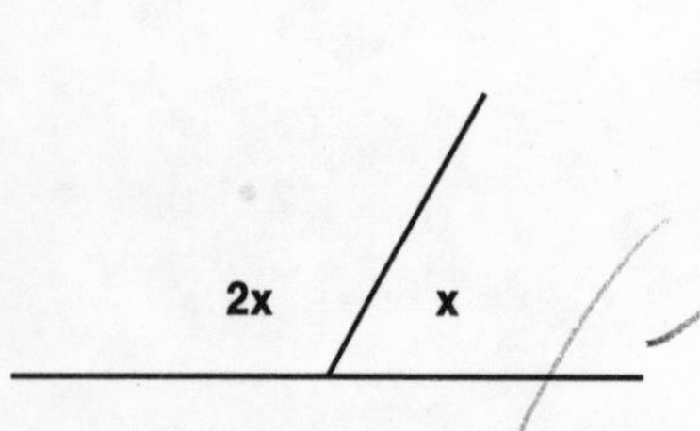

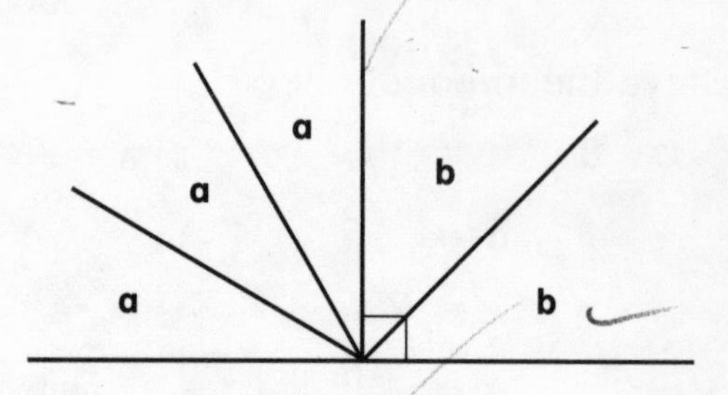

29 Angle x = 60°

30 Angle 2x = 120°

31 Angle a = 30°

32 Angle b = 45°

Complete the timetable below. There are five 40 minute lessons, with a break of 15 minutes after the 2nd lesson.

33–43		Begins	Ends
	1st lesson	09.15	09.55
	2nd lesson	09.55	10.35
	Break	10.35	10.50
	3rd lesson	10.50	11.30
	4th lesson	11.30	12.10
	5th lesson	12.10	12.50

There are 630 children in a school. There are 5 boys to every 4 girls.

44-45 There are 350 boys and 280 girls.

The perimeter of a rectangle is 40 cm. The length is 4 times the width.

46–47 The length is 16 cm and the width 4 cm

1 kg of Brightwash costs £1·20. At this price per kg:

48 For £6.00 I would get 5 kg

49 For 30p I would get 250 g

50 3·5 kg would cost £4·20

Paper 15

Write the following fractions in decimal form.

1–3 $4\frac{1}{2}$ 4·5 $3\frac{7}{10}$ 3·7 $6\frac{9}{100}$ 6·09

4–6 $7\frac{17}{100}$ 7·17 $9\frac{1}{1000}$ 9·001 $11\frac{23}{100}$ 11·23

7 After I had bought a book costing £2·40, one third of what I had left was £1·20. How much did I have at first? £6·00

There are 24 children in our class. This diagram shows how many of us belong to the Cycling Club, and how many belong to the Swimming Club.

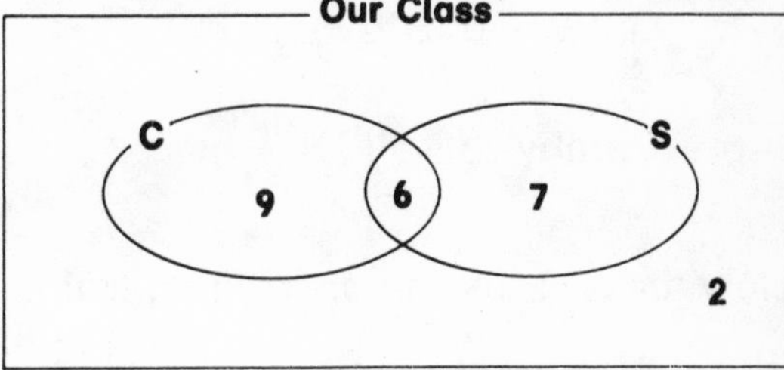

8 How many belong to the Cycling Club? 15

9 How many belong to the Swimming Club? 13

10 How many belong to both clubs? 6

11 How many belong to neither? 2

12 How many belong to one club only? 16

13 How many children don't belong to the Cycling Club? 9

14 How many don't belong to the Swimming Club? 11

This map is covered with a grid, the lines of which are numbered 0 to 6 for eastings and 0 to 6 for northings.

The position of towns is found by giving their co-ordinates e.g. Bixton is (1, 2). Some of the towns are not situated on the lines, but are inside the squares. When this is so, the co-ordinates of the bottom left-hand corner of the square are given e.g. Deepby is (2, 2).

Scale: A side of a small square represents 10 km.

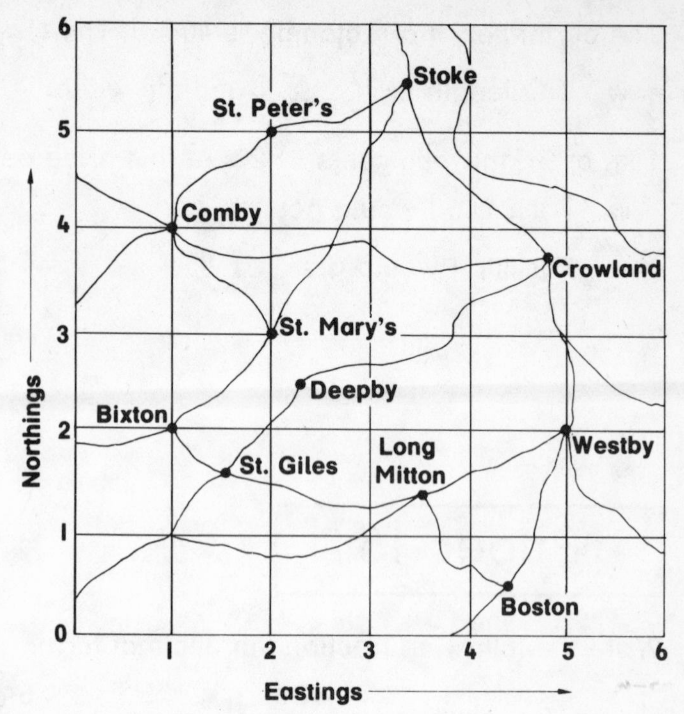

Name the towns which are at the following positions.

15 (2, 5) St. Peter's

16 (2, 3) St. Mary's

17 (3, 1) Long Mitton

18 (4, 0) Boston

Give the co-ordinates for the following towns.

19–20 Crowland (4, 3)

21–22 Westby (5, 2)

23–24 Comby (1, 4)

25–26 Stoke (3, 5)

How far is it, as the crow flies, from:

27 St. Giles to Long Mitton? 20 km

28 St. Peter's to St. Mary's? 20 km

29 St. Giles to Boston? 30 km

30 Bixton to Westby? 40 km

31 Mr. Cousins arrived at the station 7 minutes after the 17.54 train had departed. How long would he have to wait for the next train at 18.30? 29 min

There were 364 children in a school. There were 18 more girls than boys.

32 There were 191 girls. 33 There were 173 boys.

34 Take 11 from 11 thousand 10 989

Complete the following table.

		Length	Width	Area	Perimeter
35–36	Rectangle 1	7 m	4 m	28 m^2	22 m
37–38	Rectangle 2	9 m	4 m	36 m^2	26 m

Write the next two numbers in each line.

39–40 2, 5, 11, 20, 32 ... 47 65

41–42 5·7, 5·8, 6·0, 6·3 ... 6·7 7·2

43–44 $1\frac{1}{2}$, 2, $2\frac{1}{4}$, $2\frac{3}{4}$ ... 3 $3\frac{1}{2}$

45–46 0·001, 0·01, 0·1 ... 1 10

47–48 97, 86, 76, 67 ... 59 52

49–50 $\frac{1}{4}$, $\frac{3}{8}$, $\frac{1}{2}$ ... $\frac{5}{8}$ $\frac{6}{8}$ or $\frac{3}{4}$

Paper 16

Turn these 12–hour times to 24–hour clock times.

1 7.30 a.m. 07.30

2 9.05 a.m. 09.05

3 12 noon 12.00

4 1.08 p.m. 13.08

5 Find the smallest number which must be added to 890 to make it exactly divisible by 31. 9

A shop is open from 8.45 a.m. to 1 p.m., and then from 2.15 p.m. to 5.30 p.m.

6 How many hours is the shop open in one day? $7\frac{1}{2}$

7 How many hours would it be open in 5 days? $37\frac{1}{2}$

8 Find the sum of 47, 48 and 49.
Think of an easy way to do this. 144

Our school swimming bath, which is 50 m long and 20 m wide, has a path 10 m wide all round it.

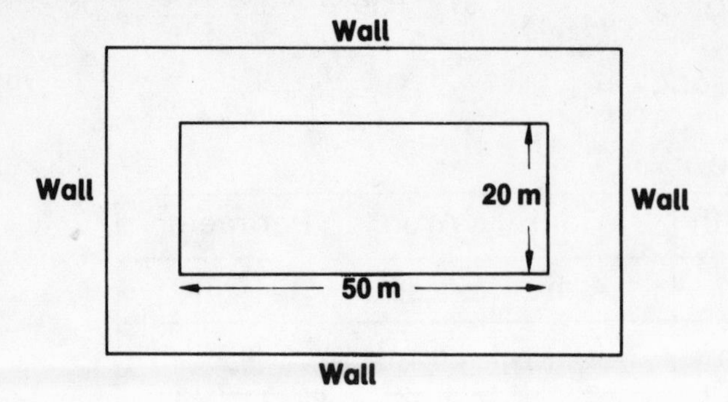

9 What is the area of the swimming bath? ....1000 m²....

10 What is the area of the whole complex (the bath and the path)? ....2800 m²....

11 What is the area of the path? ....1800 m²....

12 What is the perimeter of the bath? ....140 m....

13 What is the total length of the wall? ....220 m....

14 Mandy bought 7 metres of material. She gave the assistant £20.00 and received £2.57 change. What was the price of the material per metre? ....£2.49....

Here is a net of a model of a room, showing the walls and the floor.

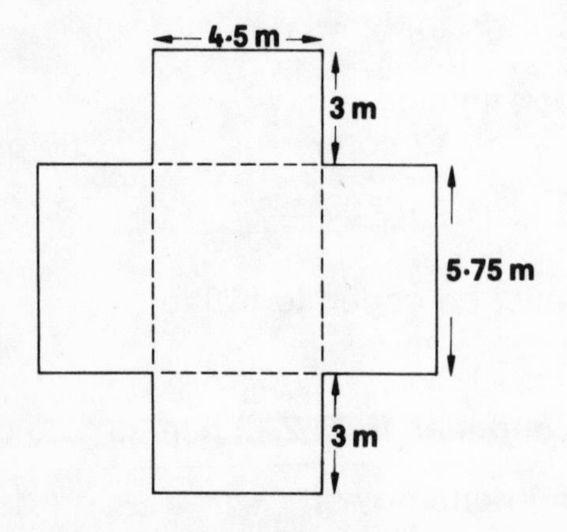

15 How high is the room? ....3 m....

16 What is the total area of the walls? ....61.5 m²....

Complete these sums:

17 $4 \times \Delta = 8 + 20$

$\Delta =$ 7

18 $\nabla \div 2 = 10 + 12$

$\nabla =$ 44

19 $3 + \nabla = 20 - 3$

$\nabla =$ 14

20 $10 - \Delta = 27 \div 3$

$\Delta =$ 1

Divide each number by 100, giving the answer in decimal form.

21 34.2	22 8.6	23 274.6	24 3
0.342	0.086	2.746	0.03

Tim, Carl and Louis together had 126 marbles. Carl won 3 from Tim, and Louis lost 2 to Carl. Then they found that Tim had twice as many as Carl, and Carl had twice as many as Louis.

25-27 Tim started the game with 75, Carl with 31 and Louis 20

28-30 At the end of the game Tim had 72, Carl 36 and Louis 18

We asked 144 children at our school how they spent their holiday. When we got their answers we made this pie chart.

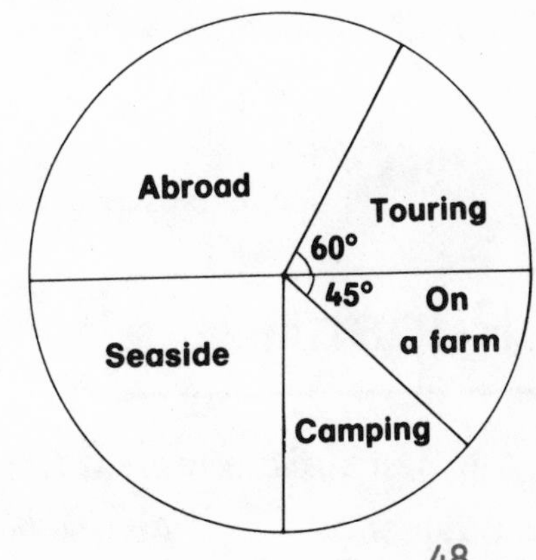

31 How many children went abroad? 48

32 How many toured? 24

33 The number of children who went to the seaside was 36

34 How many went camping? 18

35 How many went to a farm? 18

In a school there were altogether 476 pupils and teachers.

The girls + the teachers = 241 The boys + the teachers = 258

36–38 There were 23 teachers, 235 boys and 218 girls.

Underline the correct answer in each line.

39	$\frac{1}{3} + \frac{1}{6}$	$= \frac{2}{3}$	$\frac{1}{2}$	$\frac{1}{9}$	$\frac{2}{9}$	$\frac{1}{6}$
40	$\frac{1}{5} + \frac{7}{10}$	$= \frac{8}{10}$	$\frac{8}{15}$	$\frac{9}{15}$	$\frac{11}{15}$	$\frac{9}{10}$
41	111 − 19	= 100	128	102	82	92
42	6 ÷ 1.2	= 48	5	50	0.5	5.3
43	$3^3 - 5^2$	= 8	15	3	2	1
44	60 ÷ 3	= 20	4	8	32	8
45	25% of 48	= 24	48	25	12	60
46	$\frac{1}{4} \times \frac{1}{4}$	= 1	$\frac{1}{8}$	$\frac{1}{16}$	$\frac{1}{2}$	$\frac{1}{6}$

Fill in the spaces:

		Circle 1	Circle 2	Circle 3	Circle 4
47–50	Radius	3·25 cm	4·9 cm	3·15 cm	4·68 cm
	Diameter	6·5 cm	9·8 cm	6·3 cm	9·36 cm

Paper 17

Here are Ben's exam marks. Can you turn them into percentages?

	Subject	Actual mark	Possible mark	Percentage
1	Nature Study	12	15	80
2	French	21	35	60
3	English	68	80	85
4	Art	63	70	90
5	Music	14	20	70

6 Ben's total marks were 178

7 His average percentage mark was 77

Write down Peter's actual marks.

	Subject	Actual mark	Possible mark	Percentage
8	Nature Study	9	15	60
9	French	28	35	80
10	English	44	80	55
11	Art	49	70	70
12	Music	13	20	65

13 Peter's total marks were 143

14 His average percentage mark was 66

Write each of these numbers to the nearest whole number.

15 8·35 — 8 **16** 0·71 — 1 **17** 4·48 — 4 **18** 3·82 — 4

Divide 1 hour into 3 parts, the 1st part being twice as long as the 2nd and the 2nd part being 3 times as long as the 3rd.

19–21 The 1st part is 36 minutes, the 2nd part 18 minutes and the 3rd part 6 minutes.

These are nets of solids. What solids will they make?

22

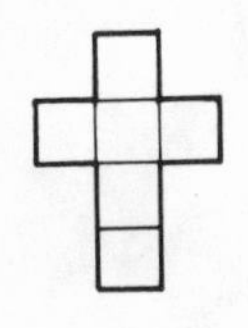

cube

23

triangular pyramid

24

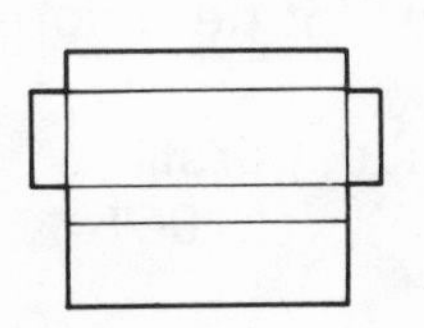

cuboid

25

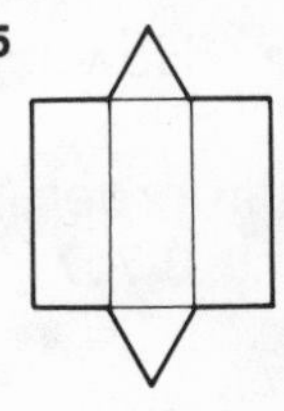

triangular prism

26

```
  7946
  5878
  6575
+ 9876
------
 30275
```

27 Write the answer to the last sum in words.

Thirty thousand two hundred and seventy-five

Complete the following chart.

		Length	Width	Perimeter	Area
28–29	Rectangle 1	29 m	1 m	60 m	29 m²
30–31	Rectangle 2	28 m	2 m	60 m	56 m²
32–33	Rectangle 3	25 m	5 m	60 m	125 m²
34–35	Rectangle 4	20 m	10 m	60 m	200 m²
36–37	Rectangle 5	15 m	15 m	60 m	225 m²

38 Multiply 0·0907 by 0·025 ..... 0·0022675

This is the time on Saturday evening.

39 How long will it be before it is midnight on Saturday? ..... 3 hr 45 min

40 How long will it be before it is 11.10 a.m. on Sunday? ..... 14 hr 55 min

41 How long will it be before it is noon on Sunday? ..... 15 hr 45 min

42 How long will it be before it is 12.20 a.m. on Sunday? ..... 4 hr 5 min

Put in order, smallest first.

0·707   0·78   0·708   0·7   0·77

43–47 0·7 ..... 0·707 ..... 0·708 ..... 0·77 ..... 0·78

48 3 numbers, when multiplied together, give 918. One number is 6 and another is 9. What is the 3rd number? 17

49 Find the length of a ladder which has 10 rungs, each pair being 30 cm apart. There is a space of 20 cm at each end of the ladder. ..... 3·1 m

50 What is the number nearest to 5000, but less than it, into which 89 will divide without remainder? 4984

Paper 18

1 In a class, 19 children have dogs, and 18 children have cats. If 15 children have both dogs and cats find the smallest possible number in the class. 22

2 How many times can 27 be subtracted from 1431? 53 times

3 12 toys were bought for £1.25 each and sold for £1.60 each. What was the total profit? £4.20

Here are some exchange rates for foreign money. Fill in the gaps.

	£	Italian lire	Austrian schillings	French francs	Dutch guilders
	1·00	2400	18	10	5
4–7	10·00	24 000	180	100	50
8–11	5·00	12 000	90	50	25
12–15	50p	1200	9	5	2·5

Arrange in order, putting the largest first:

16–19 7·8 7·088 7·88 7·008

7·88 7·8 7·088 7·008

Complete the following table.

	Fraction	Decimal	Percentage
20–21	$\frac{1}{2}$	0·5	50
22–23	$\frac{1}{4}$	0·25	25
24–25	$\frac{1}{5}$	0·2	20

Solve these equations:

26–30 $\frac{56}{a} = 8$ $\frac{49}{b} = 7$ $\frac{72}{9} = x$ $\frac{y}{4} = 3$ $\frac{z}{9} = 7$

a = 7 b = 7 x = 8 y = 12 z = 63

31 The product of two numbers is 111. The larger number is 37. What is the smaller number? 3

	Train A	Train B	Train C	Train D
Westbury	↓ 08.11	↓ 09.20	18.09 ↑	20.09 ↑
Trowbridge	08.19	09.30	17.58	20.04
Bath	08.45	09.54	17.23	19.31
Bristol	09.00	10.11	17.05	19.17

32 Which is the fastest of these trains? Train A

33 How long does this train take to travel from Westbury to Bristol? 49 min

34 Which is the slowest of the trains? Train C

35 How long does that take to do the entire journey? 1 hr 4 min

36 If I live in Westbury, and want to be in Bath before 9 a.m., on which train must I travel? Train A

37 Mrs. Gofar lives in Trowbridge and goes to Bristol to do some shopping. If she leaves on the 9.30 train and returns on the 17.05 how long does she have in Bristol? 6 hr 54 min

38 How long does the 19.31 from Bath take to travel to Westbury? 38 min

39 When should the 17.23 from Bath arrive in Westbury? 18.09

New Zealand is 12 hours ahead of our time.

India is $5\frac{1}{2}$ hours ahead of our time.

Greece is 2 hours ahead of our time.

Kenya is 3 hours ahead of our time.

Sweden is 1 hour ahead of our time.

40 When it is 10.00 a.m. in London what time is it in New Zealand? 10.00 p.m.

41 When it is 9.00 a.m. in London what time is it in India? 2.30 p.m.

42 When it is 3.30 p.m. in Greece what time is it in London? 1.30 p.m.

43 When it is 1.15 p.m. in Sweden what time is it in London? 12.15 p.m.

44 If I made a telephone call from Kenya to India at 3.00 p.m. what time would it be in India? 5.30 p.m.

	Years	months
Tony is	10	8
Claire is	9	6
Simon is	11	4
Mandy is	10	2
45 Add their ages	41	8

46 What is the average (mean) age of the four children?

..10.. years ..5.. months

Here is a box 20 cm long, 10 cm wide, and 8 cm high.

A ribbon is placed round the box, once lengthwise, and once round the width.

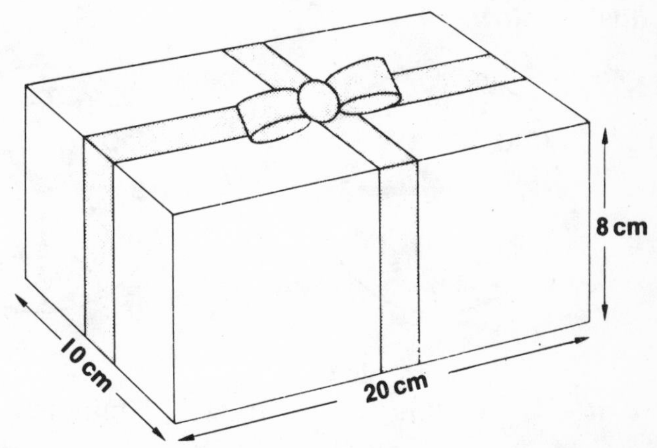

47 If I allow 35 cm for the bow, how much ribbon shall I need? ..1·27 m..

48 What is the perimeter of a long side? ..56 cm..

49 What is the perimeter of short side? ..36 cm..

50 What is the perimeter of the base of the box? ..60 cm..

Paper 19

Divide each of the numbers below by 10. Give your answers as mixed numbers, the fractions being in their lowest terms.

1 78 ..$7\frac{4}{5}$.. **2** 475 ..$47\frac{1}{2}$.. **3** 312.5 ..$31\frac{1}{4}$.. **4** 1.25 ..$\frac{1}{8}$..

5 How many metres must be added to 1·35 km to make 4 km? 2650

36 new library books are shared among Classes 1, 2 and 3, in the ratio of 2:3:4.

6–8 Class 1 gets 8 books, Class 2 12 books and Class 3 16 books.

The correct time is 12.43. The clocks are all set at the wrong time. In the space write the number of minutes they are wrong, saying if they are fast or slow.

9–10 32 minutes ~~slow~~ fast

11–12 47 minutes ~~slow~~ fast

13–14 48 minutes slow ~~fast~~

Give the answers to the following in decimal form.

15 17 tenths 1.7

16 143 hundredths 1.43

17 47 units 47.0

18 7 thousandths 0.007

19 259 tens 2590.0

20 14 hundreds 1400.0

Insert signs to make the following correct.

21–23 5 + 5 + 1 = 13 − 2

24–26 (4 × 7) − 3 = 5 × 5

27 4·9 × 100 = 490

28 1·23 ÷ 10 = 0·123

29 0·136 × 100 = 13·6

30 The average of 6 numbers is $4\frac{1}{2}$. If one of the numbers is 2, what is the average of the other 5 numbers? ....5....

VAT (Value Added Tax) is added to the price of some goods. It is charged at $17\frac{1}{2}$% (£17.50 on each £100). Complete the following table.

31–36

Price before VAT	VAT	Total price
£300	£52·50	£352·50
£150	£26·25	£176·25
£60	£10·50	£70·50

Three rectangular pieces of card have the same area (24 cm²). Fill in the other measurements.

		Length	Width	Perimeter	Area
37–38	Piece A	8 cm	3 cm	22 cm	24 cm²
39–40	Piece B	6 cm	4 cm	20 cm	24 cm²
41–42	Piece C	12 cm	2 cm	28 cm	24 cm²

43–44 What percentages are the following fractions?

$\frac{15}{30}$ = 50% $\frac{4}{25}$ = 16%

Answer the questions below by writing **Yes** or **No**.
It would help you if you ruled in the diagonals.

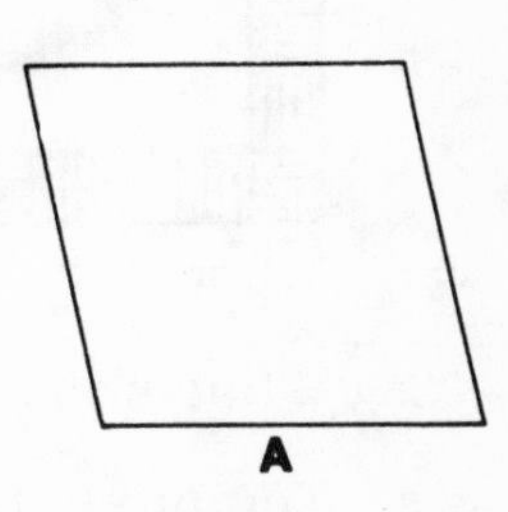

45 Are all the sides equal? ....Yes....

46 Are the opposite sides equal? ....Yes....

47 Are all the angles equal? ....No....

48 Are the diagonals equal? ....No....

49 Do the diagonals cross at right angles? ....Yes....

50 Write the set of fractions less than 1 which have a denominator of 7. $\frac{1}{7}, \frac{2}{7}, \frac{3}{7}, \frac{4}{7}, \frac{5}{7}, \frac{6}{7}$

Paper 20

Here are diagrams of two rooms. In the centre of each room there is a carpet with a border of woodblocks round it. The border in each room is 50 cm or half a metre wide.

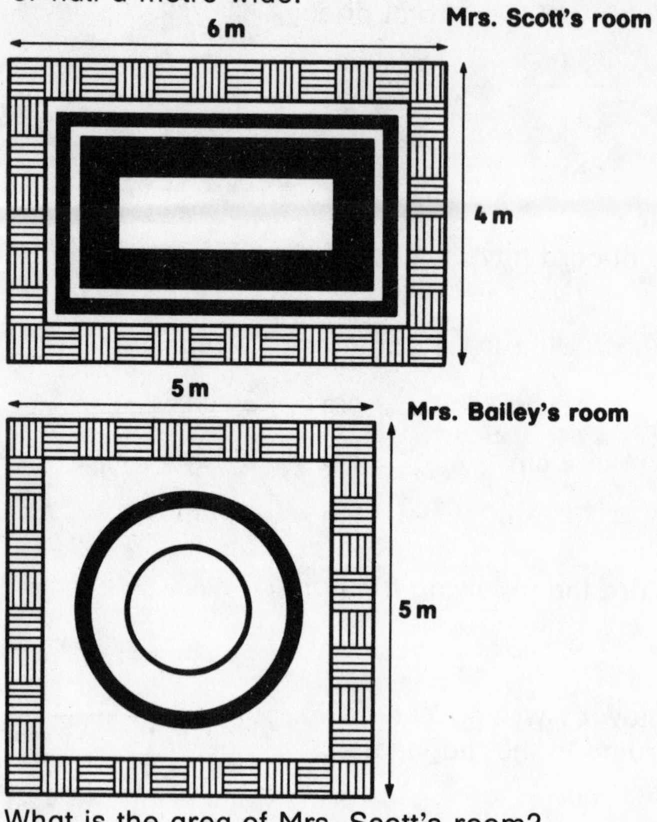

1 What is the area of Mrs. Scott's room? .... 24 m^2

2 What is the area of her carpet? .... 15 m^2

3 The area of her border is .... 9 m^2

4 What is the area of Mrs. Bailey's carpet? .... 16 m^2

5 Mrs. Scott is going to buy a fitted carpet (one to cover the entire floor). What will this cost at £11.00 a square metre? £264.00

6 What will it cost Mrs. Bailey to put a picture rail all round her room if the wood is 60p a metre? £12.00

7 In the library there were 200 books, and 58 of them were non-fiction. What percentage of the books were non-fiction? 29%

In Little Marsden the population is 17 222. The men and women together number 9142, and the women and children together number 13 201.

8–10 There are 4021 men, 5121 women and 8080 children.

11 Take 567 from one thousand. 433

12–14 Complete the figures below. The dotted line is the line of symmetry.

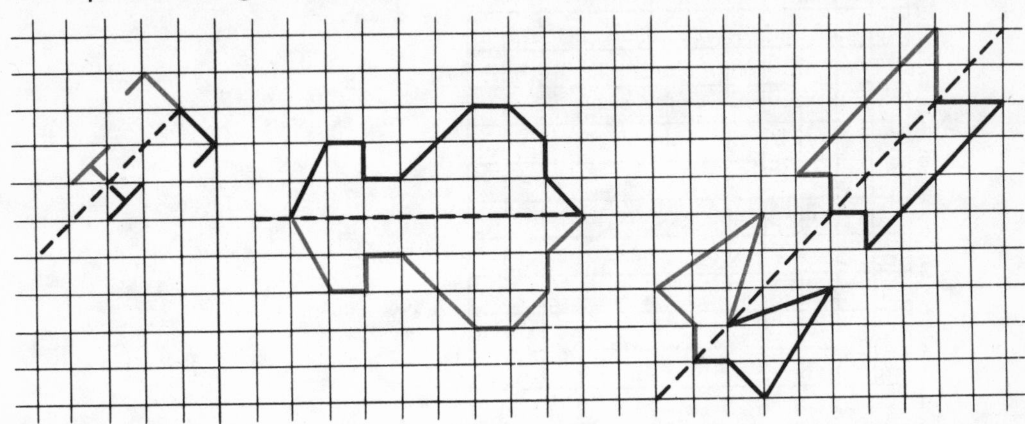

If the big hand of a clock is on 12.00, what time will it show when the angle between the two hands is:

15 180° 6 o'clock

16 30° 11 o'clock or 1 o'clock

17 120° 4 o'clock or 8 o'clock

18 60° 2 o'clock or 10 o'clock

19 150° 5 o'clock or 7 o'clock

20 90° 3 o'clock or 9 o'clock

21 In a certain sum John multiplied by 9 instead of dividing by 9. His answer was 4131. What should it have been? 51

22 $\frac{5}{8}$ of my money is £2.50. What is $\frac{2}{5}$ of it? £1.60

23 What must be added to 178·5 g to make 1 kg? 821·5 g

Put a ring round the correct answers.

24–28 $13 \times 11 =$ 132 (143) 133

$15^2 =$ 165 155 (225)

$64 =$ (8^2) 9^2 7^2

$702 \div 3 =$ 214 (234) 204

$14 \times 12 =$ 154 148 (168)

29–41 Plot these points and join them in order:

(5,1) (5,5) (2,3) (5,6) (2,5) (4,7) (6,11) (8,7) (10,5) (7,6) (10,3) (7,5) (7,1)

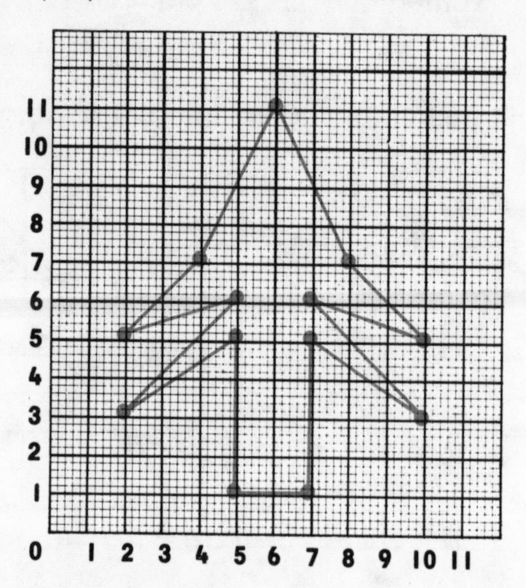

42 What have you drawn? ......a tree......

43–45 There were 227 peas in a bottle. Dad said there were $\frac{5}{12}$ of 480. Uncle Dave guessed that there were $\frac{4}{7}$ of 420, and Grandad thought there would be $\frac{3}{5}$ of 450.

......Uncle Dave...... was nearest, ...Dad...... was second

and ......Grandad...... was third.

What will be the length of a side of the squares which have the same area as the following rectangles?

	Sides of rectangle	Side of square
46	9 cm × 4 cm	6 cm
47	25 cm × 4 cm	10 cm
48	16 cm × 4 cm	8 cm

Last Friday $\frac{1}{8}$ of the children in our school were absent. There are 560 pupils altogether.

49–50 How many children were absent? ......70...... How many were present? ......490......

Paper 21

At the Manor Road car park the charges were as follows:

Up to 4 hours	£1.00
Over 4 hours and up to 5 hours	£1.50
Over 5 hours and up to 6 hours	£2.00
Over 6 hours and up to 7 hours	£2.50
Over 7 hours and up to 8 hours	£3.00
Over 8 hours and up to 9 hours	£3.50
Over 9 hours and up to 10 hours	£4.00

1 Mr. Bond's car was in the car park from 10.45 a.m. to 5.30 p.m. How much did he have to pay? £2.50

2 Mrs. Green's car was there from 11.05 a.m. to 4.45 p.m. What was she charged? £2.00

3 Mr. Rudge's car was in the park from 9.30 a.m. to 12.20 p.m. He would have to pay £1.00

4 Miss Sherlock's car was in the park from 8.40 a.m. to 5.45 p.m. She was charged £4.00

Write the following amounts correct to the nearest £1.00.

5 £2·42	6 £2·71	7 £4·59	8 £6·49	9 £7·63
£2·00	£3·00	£5·00	£6·00	£8·00

10 $\frac{2}{3}$ of a sum of money is 48p. What is $\frac{5}{8}$ of it? 45p

11 What is the whole amount? 72p

How much do the vegetables weigh?

12–17

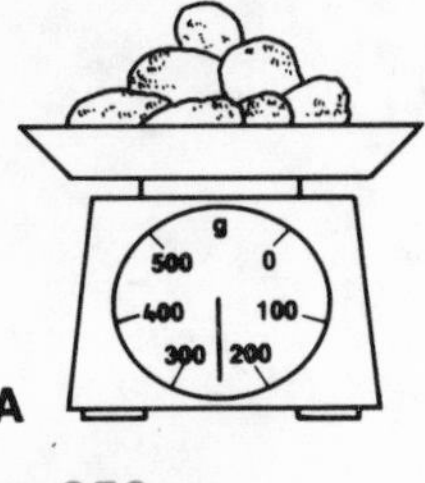

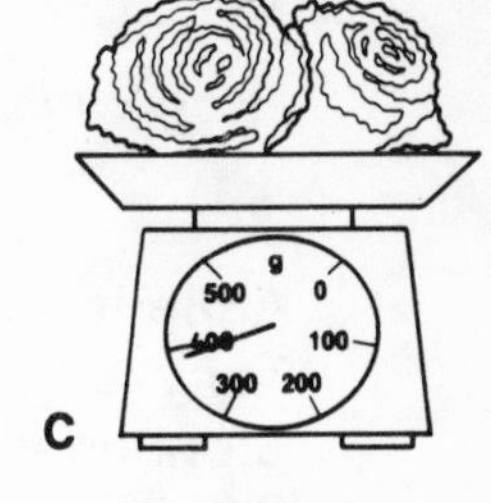

A 250 g B 160 g C 390 g

How much less than 1 kg are these three weights together? 200 g

How much more than $\frac{1}{2}$ kg are these three weights together? 300 g

Which scale shows $\frac{1}{4}$ kg? A

Divide these numbers by 100

18 374	19 14·8	20 2·55
3·74	0·148	0·0255

There are 420 children in a school. 45% of the pupils are boys.

21 How many boys are there? 189

22 How many girls are in the school? 231

£9·00 is shared between Mick, Paddy and Jake in the ratio of 8:5:2.

23–25 Mick receives £4·80

Paddy receives £3·00

Jake receives £1·20

Arrange in order, largest first:

26–30 $\frac{7}{12}$ $\frac{3}{8}$ $\frac{3}{4}$ $\frac{11}{24}$ $\frac{5}{6}$

$\frac{5}{6}$ $\frac{3}{4}$ $\frac{7}{12}$ $\frac{11}{24}$ $\frac{3}{8}$

How many points of rotational symmetry has each shape?

31–34

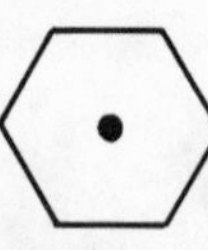

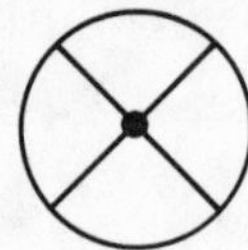

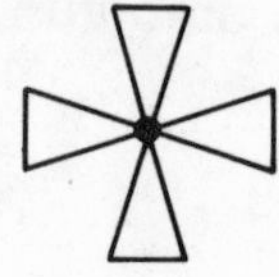

6 3 4 4

35–38

08.05 00.10 17.45

8.20 p.m. 8.05 a.m. 12.10 a.m. 5.45 p.m.

	years	months
Anne is	10	11
Tony is	10	8
Stephen is	11	4
Sally is	10	2
Elaine is	10	8
39 Total:	53	9

40 What is their average age? 10 years 9 months

We asked 72 children to name their favourite colour. We then made this pie chart.

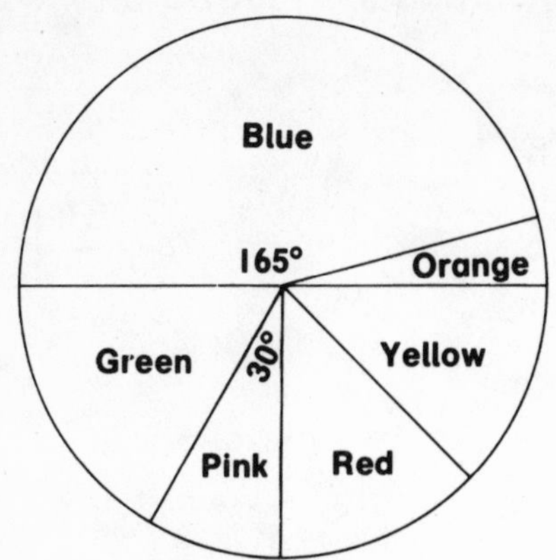

41 How many children like green best? 12

42 How many prefer blue? 33

43 How many prefer orange? 3

44 How many like red best? 9

45 The number of children who prefer pink is 6

46 How many prefer yellow? 9

Add the greatest to the smallest.

47 £$\frac{1}{2}$ £0.55 27 × 2p £$\frac{13}{25}$ £1.00 − 49p £1.05

Keith has $\frac{1}{3}$ as many marbles as Michael, and Michael has $\frac{1}{2}$ as many as Nicholas. Together they have 140.

48 Keith has 14

49 Michael has 42

50 Nicholas has 84

Paper 22

1 The school hall is 4 times as long as it is wide. If the perimeter is 55 metres, what is the length? 22 metres

2 What is the width? 5·5 metres

Ahmed had 30 sweets. $\frac{3}{5}$ of them were toffees and the rest were chocolates.
Ben had 40 sweets. $\frac{3}{8}$ of them were chocolates and the rest were toffees.

3 Who had the most toffees? Ben

4 How many more than Ahmed did he have? 7

5 Who had the most chocolates? Ben

6 He had 3 more than Ahmed .

How far can I go?
How long will it take?
What is my speed?

Complete the table below.

	Speed	Time	Distance
7–10	50 km/h	2 hr 30 min	125 km
	40 km/h	$3\frac{1}{2}$ hr	140 km
	60 km/h	$2\frac{1}{2}$ hrs	150 km
	150 km/h	20 min	50 km

Give the value of the 7 in each of the following numbers.

11 13·78 — $\frac{7}{10}$

12 37·89 — 7 units

13 378·95 — 7 tens

14–16 1 4 3 2 + 7 9 8 = 2 2 3 0 so 3 4 3 2 + 7 9 8 will be 4 2 3 0

2 4 3 2 + 1 7 9 8 will be 4 2 3 0

4 4 3 2 + 7 9 8 will be 5 2 3 0

Fill in the next two numbers in each line.

17–18	95	89	84	80	77	75
19–20	87	79	72	66	61	57
21–22	31	33	36	40	45	51
23–24	144	133	121	110	98	87
25–26	133	121	109	97	85	73

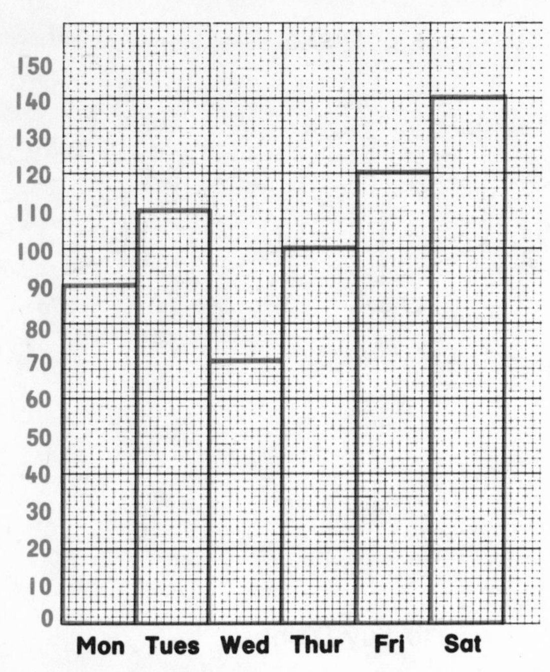

27–32 On the squared paper draw a column graph to show the following information:
The number of cups of coffee sold at Buttercup Café last week:

Monday 90
Tuesday 110
Wednesday 70
Thursday 100
Friday 120
Saturday 140

Be careful to use a scale which will show this information accurately. Write in your scale.

Here is part of a railway timetable. Fill in the times at which Train B will reach the stations. It takes exactly the same time to do the journey as Train A.

33–37

	Train A arrives at	Train B arrives at
Barwich	07.30	10.05
Hoole	07.48	10.23
Carby	08.02	10.37
Manton	08.15	10.50
Pemby	08.29	11.04
Durwich	08.54	11.29

At the supermarket there were various sizes of Disho.

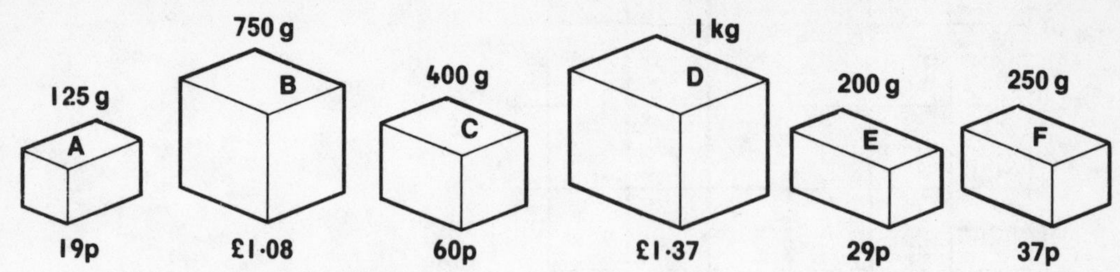

38–43 Tin D....... was the best bargain.

Tin B....... was second best.

Tin E....... was third best.

Tin F....... was fourth best.

Tin C....... was fifth best.

Tin A....... was the most expensive way to buy Disho.

44 A coil of rope was divided into 7 equal sections, each 17·5 metres long. If there were 3·25 metres left, how long was the rope? 125·75 m

45 How many days are there between 4th January and 2nd March 1995? Do not include either of the given dates. 56

46 A greenhouse can be bought by paying a deposit of £45·00, and then 12 monthly payments of £37·50. What was the total cost? £495·00

47 How many fifths are there in $12\frac{4}{5}$? 64

48 What is the smallest number into which 6, 8, 10 and 12 will all divide without remainder? 120

49 The houses on Union Street are all on one side, and are numbered 1, 2, 3, 4 and so on. If the house with the middle number is No. 37, how many houses are there in the street? 73

50 Cavby Wanderers had 8400 spectators to watch their game this week. Last week the attendance was 7000. What was the percentage increase this week? 20%

Paper 23

A = set of all tigers
B = set of all lions
C = set of all four-legged animals
D = set of zoo animals

1–3 In each of the figures below mark the second set with either B, C or D.

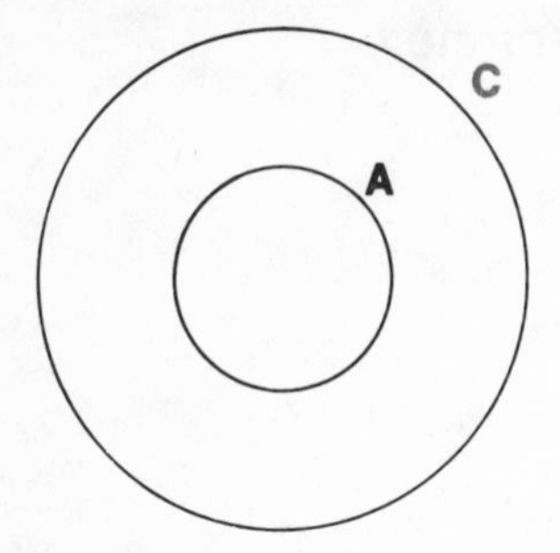

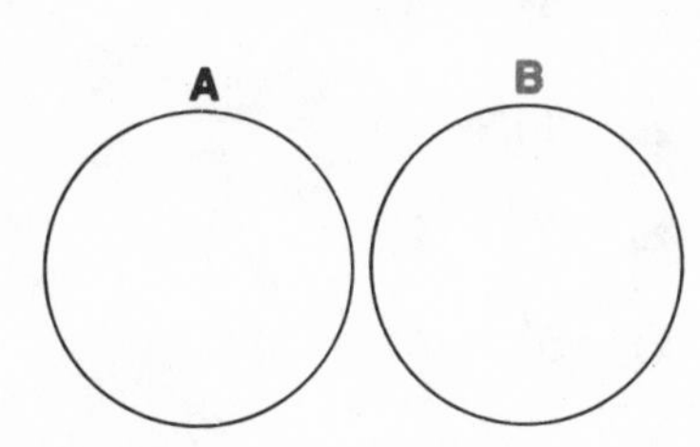

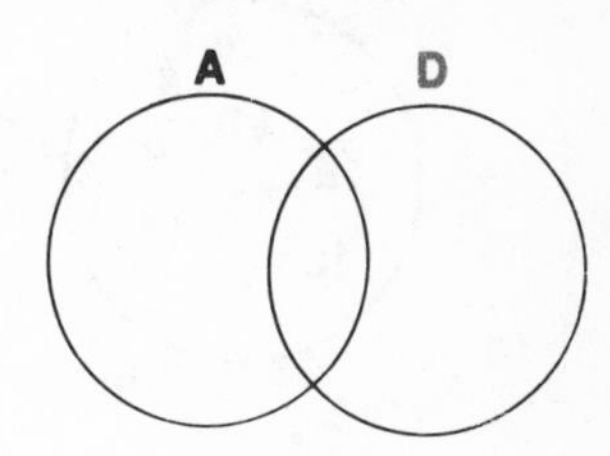

Complete the following chart. Increase all prices by 20%.

	Original price	Increased price
4	£90·00	£108·00
5	£70·00	£84·00
6	£110·00	£132·00
7	£40·00	£48·00
8	£130·00	£156·00
9	£210·00	£252·00
10	£170·00	£204·00

Write the numbers below, correct to the nearest 100.

11 71246 ....71200.... **12** 1486 ....1500.... **13** 1274 ....1300.... **14** 704·85 ....700....

15 What number is half way between 98 and 144? ....121....

At Blackhorse Junior School there were altogether 394 teachers and children. The teachers and the boys numbered 189, and the girls and teachers together numbered 219.

16–18 There were ..14.. teachers, ..175.. boys and ..205.. girls.

19 Make 478 three hundred times as large. 143 400

$\nabla = \square + 3$

Complete this table.

20–23

$\square$	0	1	2	3
∇	3	4	5	6

The answers to the questions will be found in the circle.

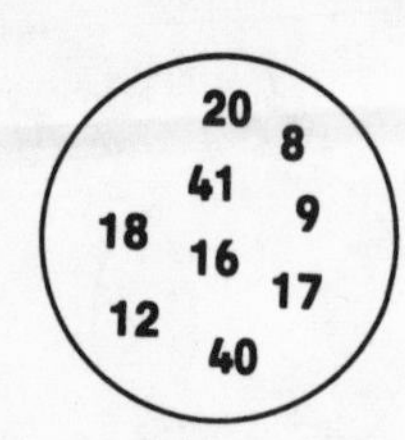

24 $9^2 - 8^2 =$ 17

25 $11^2 - 9^2 =$ 40

26 $2^3 + 2^2 =$ 12

27 $5^2 - 4^2 =$ 9

Find the area of these triangles.
The area of a triangle $= \frac{1}{2}$(base × height) 1 sq = 1 cm²

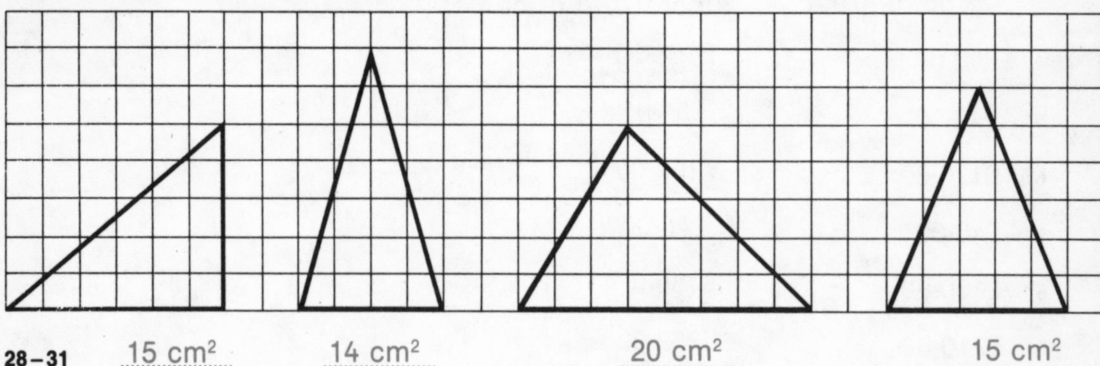

28–31 15 cm² 14 cm² 20 cm² 15 cm²

Divide the year 1985 into two parts so that the second part is 4 times as long as the first part.

32 How many days are there in the shorter part? 73 days

33 In the longer part there are 292 days.

34 If the shorter section starts on January 1st when does it end? 14th March

35 If $\frac{5}{12}$ of the contents of a box weigh 20 kg, what is the weight of all the contents? 48 kg

36 What would $\frac{1}{8}$ of the contents weigh? 6 kg

37–40 Fill in the missing numbers.

a	35	77	47	89
3a	105	231	141	267

41 By how much is the product of 27 and 13 greater than their sum? 311

42 There are 180 sheep in a flock. For every 9 white sheep there is 1 black sheep. How many white sheep are there? 162

43 How many black sheep? 18

44 Mr. Pin paid £7·05 for 1·5 metres of material. What was the cost per metre? £4·70

45 How much would 3.5 metres cost? £16·45

46 What is the next odd number after 160 into which 9 will divide without remainder? 171

Write these fractions in decimal form:

47–50 $3\frac{1}{8}$ 3·125 $4\frac{1}{20}$ 4·05 $7\frac{5}{8}$ 7·625 $9\frac{3}{40}$ 9·075

Paper 24

Underline the correct answer:

1 $\frac{1}{3} + \frac{1}{4} =$ $\frac{1}{7}$ <u>$\frac{7}{12}$</u> $\frac{2}{7}$ $\frac{2}{12}$

2 10 − 1·99 = 9·11 <u>8·01</u> 11·99 9·01

3 0·04 × 0·4 = <u>0·016</u> 0·16 0·08 0·0016

4 4 ÷ 0·02 = 20 2 0.2 <u>200</u>

5 17·89 ÷ 10 = 178·9 1789 <u>1·789</u> 17·89

6 2·7 × 200 = 5·4 <u>540</u> 54·0 0·54

7 The perimeter of a square is 28 cm. What is its area? 49 cm²

8

$$\begin{array}{r} 147 \\ \times \quad 49 \\ \hline 7203 \\ \hline \end{array}$$

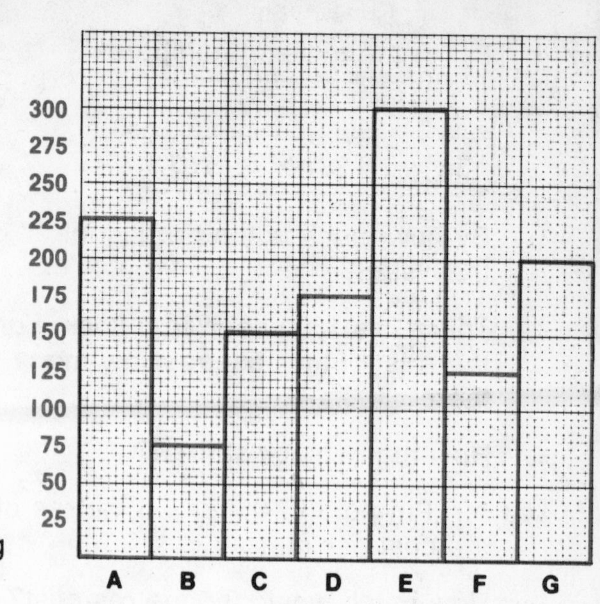

On the squared paper draw a column graph to show the following information:

9–15

Shop	A	B	C	D	E	F	G
Cameras sold	225	75	150	175	300	125	200

Be careful to use a scale which will show this information accurately. Write in your scale.

16 How many tiles, each 50 cm × 50 cm, would be needed to cover a floor 5 metres × 4 metres? 80

17 What would be the cost of these tiles if I had to pay £7·50 for 10 tiles? £60·00

Here are two Venn diagrams. Fill in the information given below in both diagrams.

P = pupils in a school = 300
H = pupils who have black hair = 59
E = pupils who have brown eyes = 127

18–20

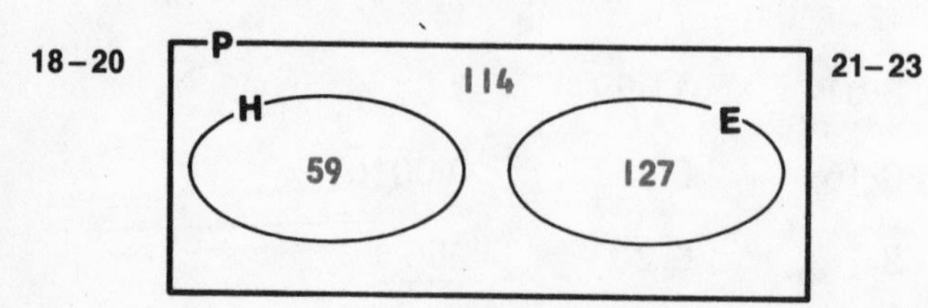

21–23

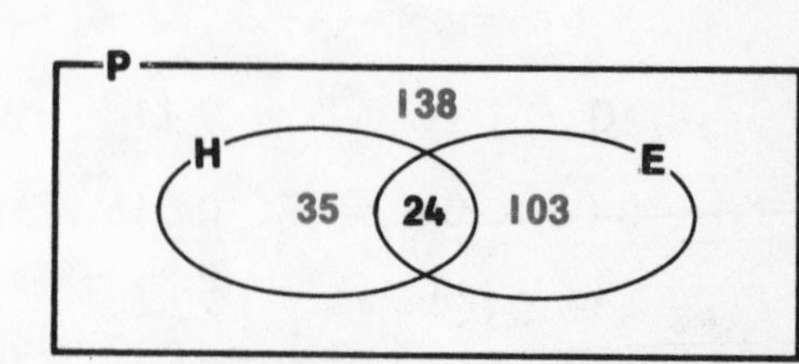

24 How many times can 34 be subtracted from 986? 29 times

25 Ted has 98p and Tom has 64p. How much must Ted give Tom so that they will each have the same amount? 17p

There are 550 children in our school. Next term the buildings are being enlarged and we will have 10% more pupils.

26 How many children will there be next term? 605

3 numbers, A, B and C multiplied together equal 1944.
A × B = 216 and A × C = 162.

27–29 A is 18, B is 12 and C is 9

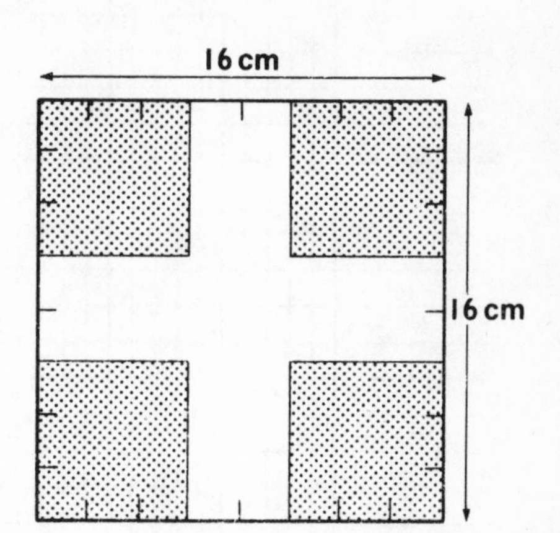

30 The area of the flag is 256 cm²

31 The area of the cross is 112 cm²

32 The shaded part has an area of 144 cm²

33 The perimeter of the flag is 64 cm

34 The perimeter of the cross is 64 cm

Complete the following:

	Fraction	Decimal	Percentage
35–36	$\frac{3}{10}$	0·3	30%
37–38	$\frac{7}{100}$	0·07	7%
39–40	$\frac{1}{4}$	0·25	25%
41–42	$\frac{1}{20}$	0·05	5%

43 8 − 1·127 6·873

44 47·625 ÷ 2·5 19.05

Complete the following table.

	Wholesale price	Retail price	Profit
45	£18.75	£23.50	£4.75
46	£58.85	£70.20	£11.35
47	£5.13	£6.10	97p
48	£196.50	£235.25	£38.75
49	£11.31	£13.50	£2.19
50	93p	£1.12	19p

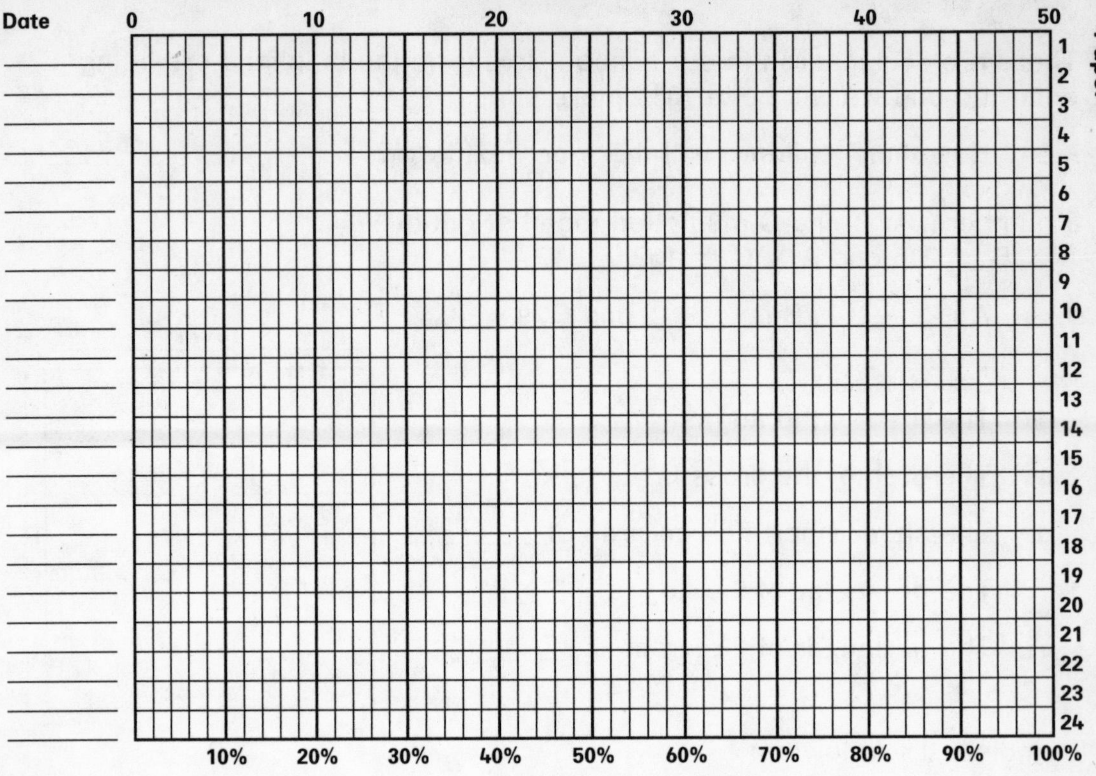

Nelson
Delta Place
27 Bath Road
Cheltenham GL53 7TH
United Kingdom

First published by Thomas Nelson and Sons Ltd 1977
Second edition 1983
Revised edition 1986
This fully revised edition 1994

Pupil's book ISBN 0-17-424507-6
NPN 10 9
Answer book ISBN 0-17-424508-4
NPN 10

By the same author

First, Second, Third, Fourth and Further Fourth Year Assessment Papers in Mathematics

First, Second, Third, Fourth and Further Fourth Year Assessment Papers in English

First, Second, Third, Fourth and Further Fourth Year Assessment Papers in Reasoning

Printed in Croatia by Zrinski d.d. Cakovec